RISKY BUSINESS

THE USE, MANAGEMENT, TRANSPORT, AND DISPOSAL OF ASBESTOS IN ONTARIO

DAVID McROBERT

CreateSpace

Charleston, South Carolina

April 2012 (Edition 1)

Cataloguing and Publication Data

McRobert, David Stanley, 1959 -

ISBN-13: 978-1470197254

ISBN: 1469939649
ISBN 13: 9781469939643

In memory of my father, Stanley Charles McRobert, who suffered terribly from respiratory difficulties in the last decade of his life, which were likely attributable to asbestos exposure in his late teens and early twenties.

Other Publications by the Author/Editor

My Municipal Recycling Program made me fat and sick: How well intentioned environmentalists teamed up with the soft drink industry to promote obesity and injure workers, Charleston, South Carolina: CreateSpace, April 2012. ISBN-13: 978-1470127466

Intervenor Funding for Public Participation in Federal Environmental Decision-Making: A Short History. Charleston, South Carolina: CreateSpace, March 2012, ISBN-13: 978-1470168445

The Roots of Biological Insanity: Hunter-gatherers, Grain-based Agriculturalists and the Human Niche, Charleston, South Carolina: CreateSpace, April 2012, ISBN-13: 978-1470102845

Arctic Sovereignty Initiatives in the Canadian North, Charleston, South Carolina: CreateSpace, March 2012, ISBN-13: 978-1468193176

Deference to the Marketplace: A Case Study of the Role of the Ontario Municipal Board in Agricultural Land Conservation, 1975-1985, Charleston, South Carolina: CreateSpace, March 2012. ISBN-13: 978-1470168490

Northern Science: Fact or Fiction?: A Despairing Optimist Looks Northward, Charleston, South Carolina: CreateSpace, March 2012, ISBN-13: 978-1470028930

The Costs of the Car: A Preliminary Study of the Environmental and Social Costs Associated with Private Car Use in Ontario, Charleston, South Carolina: CreateSpace, March 2012, ISBN-13: 978-1470018184

Bureaucratic Speed Bumps and Ecological Tread Marks, Charleston, South Carolina: CreateSpace, February 2012.

Contents

1.0 Executive summary   1

2.0 Asbestos use and risks   5

3.0 Canadian federal asbestos controls   15

4.0 Ontario's environmental controls on asbestos   19

5.0 Ontario's Occupational Health & Safety controls on asbestos   27

6.0 Conclusion   33

About the Author   35

Appendix 1   Tips for homeowners on the management
               of asbestos waste   37

Appendix 2   Health risks related to asbestos exposure   41

Appendix 3   How the *EBR* applies to asbestos
               handling and asbestos risks   45

Appendix 4   MOE's waste management
               procedures to prevent asbestos exposure   49

Appendix 5   Releases of asbestos by NPRI-listed
               facilities in Ontario   55

Appendix 6   Glossary and abbreviations   57

Appendix 7   The role of mirror laws   63

Appendix 8   A proposed process for policy and law reform   67

Appendix 9   Environmental Commissioner Of Ontario,
Review of Application, R2006003: Application
for Review of RRO 1990, Regulation 347 made
under the *EPA* (Review denied by MOE),
Prepared by D. McRobert, ECO Annual Report
Supplement, 2006-07.   69

References   73

Endnotes   79

Preface and Acknowledgments

This guide was inspired in part by lectures and seminars I attended at Trent University as a Biology student in the late 1970s. My interest in the regulation of asbestos in Canada was further inspired by the editors of Alternatives Magazine, a path-breaking publication which was based at Trent for more than 10 years and edited by Trent Professor Bob Paehlke, undoubtedly one of the most sophisticated and good-humoured analysts of environmental politics and regulation in North America. Contributors including Professor Paehlke presented critical reviews of fairly pathetic federal and provincial laws, regulations, and policies that governed the use, management, containment/removal, transport, and disposal of asbestos in Canada and helped to shape our awareness of the need for significant law and policy reform.

My interest continued to grow as I continued my studies for my Masters of Environmental Studies degree at York University between 1981 and 1984. However, it was the discovery of loose or friable asbestos in the ceiling of the basement work areas of Osgoode Hall Law School at York that truly galvanized my resolve that proper management of asbestos was a very important public policy issue. In the late fall of 1986 a group of students from Osgoode, many like myself a Division Leader or student volunteer associated with the Community Legal Aid Student Program at Osgoode (CLASP), began to meet to discuss the implications of the asbestos problem at Osgoode. Communication began with the Osgoode and York Administrations, headed by Osgoode Dean John McCamus and former Dean Harry Arthurs and then York President, an expert on labour relations and a labour arbitrator. As students our primary concern was for the welfare of the maintenance and support staff working in the photocopying and materials distribution rooms, the library and other areas where the asbestos had been used in construction in the late 1960s. We knew that our days at the institution would be limited, unless one of us was appointed to the rarified role of a full Osgoode professor and that, even so, most professors did not spend as much time in the building as the regular employees.

After months of fairly fruitless exchanges, we organized a successful one-day student boycott of classes in late March 1987, marching in front of the law school with protest signs poking fun at our aspirations to become successful lawyers. One of our standard signs, which was featured on the cover of the Toronto Star the next day, proclaimed that Osgoode students "Dying to become Lawyers". Cute, we knew. But also a massive exaggeration of the risk we faced as law students.

I can happily report that later in the spring of 1987 President Arthurs and the York University Senate cried "uncle" – we had won our campaign for removal of loose asbestos in those work areas that posed the greatest risk to the regular Osgoode staff. The men in the white Hazardous Materials (Haz Mat) suits began to arrive in July of 1987.

Since that time I have been extremely fortunate to work in various Ontario government ministries and agencies including the Workplace Health and Safety Agency (WHSA), Ministry of Labour, the Ministry of the Environment, the Environmental Commissioner of Ontario (ECO), and the Ministry of the Attorney General and with non-government organizations such as Pollution Probe. All of these experiences have helped to expand my knowledge of issues related to asbestos management and handling in Ontario.

Many people helped to make this report a reality. The following individuals provided invaluable contributions to this report, through interviews, advice, and guidance: Dr. Laurie McRobert (Toronto); the editors and staff at CreateSpace; Dr. James Brophy (Sarnia); and former Osgoode Harry Glasbeek; Eric Tucker; and Judy Fudge. Magdalene Boilard and Carol Jones's EBR application filed with the ECO in 2006 (see Appendix 9 attached) was the principal inspiration behind this report but the sudden heart attack of my father, Stan McRobert, on December 24, 2007 provided a further incentive to complete the project. In addition, it almost goes without saying that such a guide is necessary amidst the growing controversy and confusion related to asbestos management and the current policies of the federal government of Canada to promote asbestos export to developing nations such as India.[1]

Special thanks to Bill Glenn and Bev Edwards for their helpful guidance, feedback, and suggestions for improving various elements of this report in early 2010.

All mistakes in this book should be blamed on the author. However, while I worked at the Ministry of Labour and the WHSA on policy and regulatory issues I feel I can take little responsibility for gaps in law and policy and poor enforcement of our occupational health and safety (OHS) laws and regulations in Ontario.

While I have dedicated this book to my late father, this book is an effort to clarify how asbestos laws apply in workplaces and community settings. I pray and hope that all those suffering from asbestos illnesses can take comfort in the fact this little book should increase awareness about risks and hopefully enhance community power. As Bob Sass once famously observed about occupational health and safety law and policy in Canada, "knowledge is not power, power is power."[2]

Yours in workplace and community health and safety,
David McRobert, Peterborough, February 2012

1.0 Executive summary

This guide reviews the federal and provincial laws, regulations, and policies that govern the proper use, management, containment/removal, transport, and disposal of asbestos and asbestos waste in Ontario. It also outlines the public's right to provide input on these activities through the avenues provided by various laws, including Ontario's *Environmental Protection Act (EPA)*, the *Occupational Health and Safety Act (OHSA)*, the *Canadian Environmental Protection Act (CEPA)*, the Workplace Hazardous Material Information System (WHMIS), the *Environmental Bill of Rights (EBR)*, and other laws. This guide also discusses ongoing public concern about the potential human health risks associated with the removal or accidental dislodging of asbestos materials in buildings and other structures, as well as the handling and disposal of used products that may contain asbestos.

Provincial jurisdiction over the management of asbestos risks is generally shared between the Ontario Ministry of the Environment (MOE) and the Ministry of Labour (MOL). In the past fifteen years, tens of thousands of Ontario residents have contacted the MOL, MOE, and various other federal, provincial, and municipal agencies to request information about asbestos and the risks and disposal because of their concerns about the handling of asbestos by contractors or spouses working in their homes or private businesses or construction or maintenance workers working in large public or private sector industrial, commercial or institutional settings. The inhalation of airborne asbestos fibers—whether in the workplace or at home—can result in a number of serious diseases, including asbestosis, malignant mesothelioma (a type of cancer), lung cancer, and other forms of cancer. As a result, the federal and provincial governments have passed a number of laws designed to minimize the public's exposure to asbestos, both in the workplace and the general environment.

The primary objective of the MOE's regulations and policies is to protect the environment and human health by preventing the release of asbestos fibers into the environment. According to RRO 1990, Reg. 347, s. 17 (Waste Management—General) made under the *EPA*, every person involved in the transportation, handling, or management of asbestos waste "shall take all precautions necessary to prevent asbestos waste from becoming airborne." The MOE sets limits on environmental release of asbestos from mining, manufacturing, and other industrial sources and oversees the proper handling, containment, transport, and disposal of asbestos waste. MOE policy also covers the excavation and removal of asbestos waste from landfills, tailing disposal areas, and industrial properties. The MOE requires—under the *Toxics Reduction Act, 2009* and its regulation, O. Reg. 455/09—that regulated facilities track and quantify the toxic substances that they use (such as asbestos) in order to develop plans for reducing the formulation and use of those substances and to make summaries of their plans available to the public.

The MOL administers occupational health and safety statutes, regulations, and policies that cover the safe handling of asbestos and asbestos-containing products in the workplace; short-term and time-weighted exposure limits; the medical screening and ongoing surveillance of potentially exposed workers; the reporting of asbestos-related illnesses arising from occupational exposure to asbestos; and the issuance of worker's compensation and other benefits in the event of disease.

The *OHSA* is the main law governing workplace health and safety in the province. O. Reg. 278/05 (Asbestos on Construction Projects and in Buildings and Repair Operations), which is part of the act, provides clear and detailed requirements for the management of asbestos in buildings and during construction and renovation. It covers the repair, alteration, or maintenance of buildings (which includes structures, vaults, chambers, and tunnels), as well as the demolition of machinery, equipment, aircraft, ships, locomotives, railway cars, and vehicles.

As of July 1, 2010, Ontario's newly-consolidated designated substances regulation (O. Reg. 490/09) addresses workplace exposure to asbestos in fixed-place operations, including asbestos mining; the crushing, grinding, or sifting of asbestos; and the processing, adaptation, or use of asbestos in the manufacture or assembly of goods and products. In addition, O. Reg. 490/09 may, in certain circumstances, apply to the repair, alteration, or maintenance of machinery, equipment, aircraft, ships, locomotives, railway cars, and vehicles.

The federal government also plays a role through restrictions on the use of asbestos in certain products and applications; requirements for product labeling; limits on environmental releases from the asbestos mining and milling sector; the collection of data on annual releases, discharges, and disposal of asbestos; and minimum standards for workplace exposures.

While occupational exposures remain the primary cause of asbestos-related disease, there have been some historical shifts in the source(s) of those exposures. Workplace exposure has been decreased dramatically in many industries through improved safety equipment and handling protocols. In certain sectors, asbestos exposure has been totally eliminated through process changes and by substituting alternatives to asbestos.

Despite these measures, current and former workers in asbestos mining and milling, construction and demolition, automotive repair, manufacturing, etc., continue to dominate the annual statistical compilation of occupational illnesses and fatalities. Prior occupational exposure to asbestos fibers accounts for about one-third of the industrial deaths registered in Canada each year.

Asbestos is still the number-one reported cause of industrial disease fatalities, and it is expected to remain so for years. This is due to the long latency periods between occupational exposure, the manifestation of symptoms, and the diagnosis of disease (such as asbestosis and malignant mesothelioma). In addition asbestosis victims may live for a number of years following the first onset of symptoms.

It is likely that the incidence of asbestosis may have peaked and will slowly decrease over several decades. However the number of mesothelioma-related deaths continues to increase in Canada and is not expected to peak for five to ten years. Neither disease is likely to be completely eradicated due to ongoing exposure to asbestos and a number of other asbestos-containing products in existing buildings.

Many medical experts state that there is no safe level of exposure. Prolonged and cumulative exposure to low levels of asbestos—or even one poorly handled remediation or asbestos removal project—could produce exposures that result in the development of fatal asbestos-related diseases.

Under Ontario law, asbestos removal contractors must be licensed, but homeowners are not prohibited from performing asbestos-related work. Such work can be extremely risky for both the homeowner and his or her family. The safe removal of asbestos from homes—especially sprayed or troweled-on asbestos insulation—requires proper training in the correct procedures and safeguards, the latest information, and special equipment (including personal protective equipment).

In some cases, it may be advisable to leave certain materials—such as insulation products that contain an asbestos component—in place; in other cases, deteriorating or friable asbestos should be removed. In *every* case, it is advisable to obtain the expert opinion of a licensed asbestos removal contractor. There are many specialized waste management companies and environmental remediation contractors who are experts in handling and removing asbestos.

Do-it-yourself asbestos removal could prove very costly. You could compromise the health of your family, leading to disability or disease, and any short-term economic savings achieved could seem trivial in hindsight.

2.0 Asbestos use and risks

The human health risks associated with the improper handling of asbestos and asbestos wastes—both by individuals and contractors—are a significant concern for many members of the public. The risks have been well-known since the 1930s. Asbestos has been regulated in Ontario, to varying degrees, for more than fifty years. However the modern era of asbestos regulation commenced in the late 1970s when the *OHSA* was enacted by the Ontario government and the MOE began to implement the *EPA* and its regulations on waste management and handling.

Asbestos is the generic name given to a family of fibrous silicate minerals used in a wide variety of commercial products. The term *asbestos* includes the following minerals: chrysotile, crocidolite, amosite, anthophyllite asbestos, tremolite asbestos, and actinolite asbestos. Since asbestos can withstand corrosive chemicals and does not ignite when exposed to high temperatures, it was very widely used in North America as an insulating and fireproofing substance. It has been estimated that 300 million tons of asbestos were mined in the twentieth century worldwide.

Today nearly all of the asbestos produced worldwide is chrysotile. While Canadian production numbers have dropped precipitously since the 1970s, Canada is still a major producer of chrysotile asbestos fiber and asbestos products. Due to the closure of the Baie Verte, Newfoundland, asbestos mining operation in 1994, Canadian chrysotile production is now concentrated in Quebec's eastern townships at the Lac d'Amiante mine (owned by LAB Chrysotile, Inc.) Two other operations—the Bell and Jeffrey mines—have suspended operations in recent years; it is uncertain if one or both will ever reopen. As of 2006, an estimated 175,000–200,000 tons of Canadian chrysotile asbestos fibers were produced and sold in domestic and international markets. In 2006, approximately 92 percent of Canadian chrysotile asbestos production (161,000 tons) was exported.

Some estimates from 2008 and 2009 suggest that Canada supplies approximately 8 percent of the world's asbestos fibre and is the world's fifth-largest producer. Along with production from Brazil (230,000 tons), China (350,000 tons), Colombia (10,000 tons), Kazakhstan (241,000 tons), Russia (1,120,000 tons) and Zimbabwe (110,000 tons), world production totaled 2,236,000 tons in 2006. However high production, energy, and transportation costs—combined with a stronger Canadian dollar—are seriously hampering the ability of the Canadian chrysotile industry to compete internationally with other producers. At the same time, a number of traditional markets have banned or restricted the uses of asbestos products. This trend is expected to continue.

According to Natural Resources Canada, countries that still permit the use of chrysotile asbestos have resident corporations or agencies which process and designate more than 93 percent of it to the chryso-cement industry and the remaining 7 percent is split into thirds: one-third into specialty products and two-thirds into friction products.

Asbestos is used mainly in building materials, shingles and roofing materials, paper products, asbestos-cement products, brakes and friction products, textiles, packings, and gaskets, and asbestos-reinforced plastics. Asbestos has been used in more than three thousand commercially manufactured products, including:

- thermal insulation (pipe and boiler insulation);
- fireproofing materials (sprayed insulation, fire door insulation);
- asbestos cement (roof and wall claddings);
- decorative and acoustic applications;
- friction materials (brake linings);
- paints, coatings, sealants, vinyl floor coverings and adhesives;
- textiles (woven cloths, socks, and blankets); and
- other miscellaneous products.[3]

Types of Asbestos		
Compound	CAS #	Properties
Actinolite	12172-67-7	straight, single, or composite fibers
Amosite	12172-73-5	a prismatic, lamellar to fibrous crystal structure; ash gray, greenish, or brown with a vitreous, somewhat pearly luster; fairly resistant to acids
Anthophyllite	17068-78-9	a prismatic, lamellar to fibrous crystal structure; gray-white, brown, gray, or green in color, with a vitreous to pearly luster; fairly resistant to acids
Chrysotile	12001-29-5	common minerals found in commercial grades include magnetite, chromite, brucite, calcite, dolomite, and awaruite; crystal structure is fibrous and asbestiform; white, gray, green, or yellowish, with a silky luster; soluble in acid
Crocidolite	12001-28-4	fibrous crystal structure; lavender or blue, with a silky dull luster; fairly resistant to acids
Tremolite	14567-73-8	straight, single, or composite fibers

Table 1-1 – Types of Asbestos.

Asbestos use in many commercially-manufactured products has been phased out in North America in the past twenty years. For example asbestos was widely used in many automotive applications (such as brake linings for cars and trucks between 1908 and the early 1990s).[4] Today other braking systems have become popular for motor vehicles, and asbestos is less widely used. In Canada non-encapsulated products (which are likely to release free fibers into the environment under normal conditions of use) are regulated or prohibited under the federal *Hazardous Products Act (HPA)*.

How and when does asbestos exposure take place?

Thousands of buildings constructed in Canada between 1930 and the late 1970s still contain asbestos insulation (often in sprayed form). This material may be released and become airborne when disturbed during maintenance work, repairs, or renovations.

Dry asbestos that can be crushed or crumbled with the hands is called *friable* asbestos. Friable asbestos is often hazardous because asbestos fibers are easily released into the air from impact and deterioration. In contrast some asbestos is bound with other materials, in products such as roofing shingles, concrete piping, or vinyl-asbestos floor tiles. Asbestos fibers are not as easily released from these products. However fibers in bound asbestos products and construction material may be released when the material is cut, drilled, or sanded, or when it begins to deteriorate due to exposure to the elements.

Exposure to asbestos occurs when asbestos fibers of various sizes are released into the air and are inhaled. In North America, most exposures occur in the workplace. The smaller fibers can remain suspended in air for long periods. These fibers are so small that they are usually only visible with a microscope. You would have to bundle approximately six hundred asbestos fibers together to equal the thickness of a single human hair.[5]

Some larger asbestos fibers may lodge in the nasal lining and upper airways, but the smaller fibers travel through the upper airways and become embedded in the lungs. The body has no effective mechanism for removing these deeply-embedded fibers.

The length, diameter, and chemical composition of fibers, as well as the duration of exposure and individual susceptibility, all have an impact on subsequent health. Malignant mesothelioma (which is considered the signature disease of asbestos exposure) is rarely associated with chrysotile asbestos exposure alone; a history of exposure to amphibole (usually crocidolite) or amphibole-chrysotile mixtures is common. Asbestosis has been associated with high and cumulative exposures to all forms of asbestos fiber.

Research indicates that the most dangerous airborne asbestos fibers are between 5-8 microns (µm) in length and thinner than 1.5 microns; these have a greater propensity to become lodged in the alveoli of the lungs.[6] The strength and durability of the fiber affects the amount of damage to the lungs. If the body's normal lung clearance mechanisms are overwhelmed due to the quantity of fibers or impaired by other activities (such as smoking), this can significantly increase the risk of disease.

What are the health risks related to asbestos exposure?

Several types of disease can result from asbestos exposure. The health hazards associated with asbestos depend on the type and dimensions of the fibers and the way in which the asbestos is used.[7] In its publications and guidelines on asbestos, the MOL notes that excessive occupational exposure to airborne respirable asbestos fibers can lead to the following diseases: asbestosis, mesothelioma, plural plaques, lung cancer, and other forms of cancer (for further information, see Appendix 2).

According to Schedule 4 of the General Regulation (O. Reg. 175/98) to the *Workplace Safety and Insurance Act*, any occurrence of either asbestosis or a primary malignant neoplasm of the mesothelium of the pleura (lining of the chest) or peritoneum (lining of the abdominal cavity) in an employee of a mining, milling, manufacturing, assembling, construction, repair, alteration, maintenance, or demolition process involving the generation of airborne asbestos fibers is irrefutably presumed to be work-related.

Is short-term exposure a risk?

There is some evidence that short-term exposure to asbestos can be harmful and cause disease. For example family members of asbestos workers have contracted asbestos-related disease from exposure to asbestos fibers on the workers' clothing.[8] Many experts believe that there is no safe level of exposure, although the higher the exposure to asbestos, the higher the risk of disease. The primary route of exposure is through inhalation; existing scientific literature does not confirm that ingesting small amounts of asbestos fibers causes chronic diseases.

What are the trends in asbestos-related disease?

The average latency period for the development of asbestos-related disease in exposed individuals can be very long—often ranging from ten to forty years, depending on the illness. This extended latency period has made it difficult to compile epidemiological statistics linking asbestos exposure to the development of subsequent illness.[9] However it has become clear that asbestos is a carcinogenic agent; that chronic exposure may result in other debilitating lung diseases; and that the greater the exposure over time, the greater the possibility of becoming ill.

In Canada asbestos exposure accounted for at least 340 deaths in 2005, 61 percent of deaths from occupational diseases, and 31 percent of total workplace fatalities. The fatality rate from asbestos has increased dramatically from 0.4 per 100,000 workers in 1996 to 2.1 per 100,000 workers in 2005. Occupations that reveal an elevated incidence of asbestos-related disease and fatality include asbestos mining and milling, automotive mechanics, construction trades, and manufacturing.

Asbestos is responsible for the lion's share of an overall increase in the incidence of Canadian occupational disease fatalities in that period. Between 1996 and 2005, the number of deaths attributable to neoplasms, tumors, and cancer increased almost six-fold—from sixty-three to 377 deaths. Deaths from asbestos-related diseases accounted for 90 percent of the deaths in this disease category in 2005.

Across Canada the number of deaths from mesothelioma increased by 17 percent from 2000 to 2003. According to Cancer Care Ontario, the number of new mesothelioma cases in Ontario increased by 260 percent over a twenty-year period—from twenty in 1982 to seventy-two in 2002.

Although occupational exposure has declined significantly, the number of asbestos-related deaths continues to climb for two reasons: (1) the long latency period of ten to forty years between exposure and the manifestation of the first debilitating symptoms; and (2) the fact that many asbestosis victims may live with the disease for a number of years before succumbing.

In the United States, the National Institute for Occupational Safety and Health (NIOSH) has tracked asbestosis deaths since 1968 and malignant mesothelioma deaths since 1999. From the late 1960s to the late 1990s, the number of asbestosis deaths increased almost twentyfold and appear to have peaked at approximately 1,500 deaths per year since 2000. NIOSH data for malignant mesothelioma are not as extensive, although they reveal that the number of annual deaths continues to increase—from 2,484 in 1999 to 2,704 in 2005.

While it appears likely that the incidence of asbestosis has peaked and will slowly decrease over several decades, the incidence of mesothelioma in Canada might not peak until sometime between 2015 and 2019—ten to fifteen years after the United States and five to ten years after Great Britain. The number of cases will then begin to decline as well.

However neither disease is likely to be completely eradicated in Canada due to ongoing exposure to asbestos in the existing building stock and a number of other asbestos-containing products. While a number of countries have banned all use of asbestos, Canada has continued to permit the use of certain asbestos products for specified applications under strictly controlled conditions.

Worldwide, the International Labour Organization (ILO) estimates that as many as one hundred thousand workers die of asbestos-related diseases every year and that these numbers are expected to grow, especially as asbestos use continues to shift toward newly-industrialized and third world nations.

Who is at greatest risk of exposure?

According to most experts, exposure to asbestos fibers is still predominantly an occupational risk rather than an environmental risk. Incidental exposure of the general population to asbestos fibers from environmental sources in the air, water, or food is relatively small.

According to the MOL, asbestos-removal workers and maintenance workers are at greatest risk of exposure to respirable dust and asbestos fibers because these may be released during their work duties. To reduce their risk of exposure, the MOL has developed a range of regulatory requirements, such as special job-site enclosures, personal protective clothing, masks and respirators, and hygiene procedures. These are intended to protect specialized workers from exposure to the dust and fibers released by asbestos disturbance or removal activities.

In the 1970s, public health authorities in Ontario, the media, and the general public became concerned about the health effects of asbestos materials on building occupants. To determine whether public anxiety related to asbestos materials in buildings was justified, the Ontario government appointed the Royal Commission on Matters of Health and Safety Arising from the Use of Asbestos in Ontario (RCA) in 1981.

The RCA concluded that asbestos does not pose a significant risk for the general occupants of a building, except in certain rare circumstances.[10] Thus it was "rarely necessary to take corrective action in buildings containing asbestos insulation in order to protect the general occupants of those buildings." The RCA further noted that air sampling undertaken by consultants had revealed that airborne asbestos levels in buildings with sprayed asbestos are no higher than outdoor levels—unless the friable asbestos or asbestos debris is disturbed at the time of sampling.[11]

While occupational exposures remain the primary cause of asbestos-related disease, there have been some historical shifts in the source(s) of those exposures. Workplace exposures have been cut dramatically in many industries through improved personal protection equipment and handling protocols. In certain sectors, asbestos exposure has been totally eliminated through process changes and the substitution of alternatives to asbestos. As discussed above, the extended latency period of up to forty years before symptoms of asbestos-related disease manifest themselves means that employees and former employees in a number of formerly dangerous job categories—asbestos mining and milling, construction and demolition, automotive repair, manufacturing, etc.—will continue to dominate the annual compilation of occupational-related disease statistics.

Due to the control of occupational sources of asbestos exposure, attention is beginning to shift to environmental sources (i.e., household and neighborhood sources). For example, a 2000 review published in the *European Journal of Epidemiology* estimates the risk of developing pleural mesothelioma (mesothelioma is considered the signature diagnostic to determine past asbestos exposure) from environmental exposure to relatively high levels of asbestos. Incidence rates ranged between 4.0 and 23.7, with a summary risk estimate of 8.1.[12] The authors suggest a substantial increase in risk of pleural mesothelioma following high environmental exposure to asbestos; however the available data is insufficient to estimate the magnitude of the excess risk at the levels of environmental exposure commonly encountered by the general population in industrial countries.

It should also be noted that some of the substitutes for asbestos pose significant health risks, especially some of the manmade mineral and vitreous fibers. "Asbestos-free" does not mean "risk-free." According to Natural Resources Canada, "substitutes that tend to be technically equivalent to chrysotile also tend to have similar properties. This means that, generally speaking, they are also fibrous and may pose similar threats to health as chrysotile and even amphibole asbestos in some cases."

Users of these alternatives—especially some of the manmade vitreous fibers (including glass wool and refractory ceramic fibers)—must conform to the relevant workplace standards, train workers about the attendant risks and proper precautions, post material safety data sheets (MSDS), and follow the manufacturer's directions in the use, handling, and disposal of these materials.

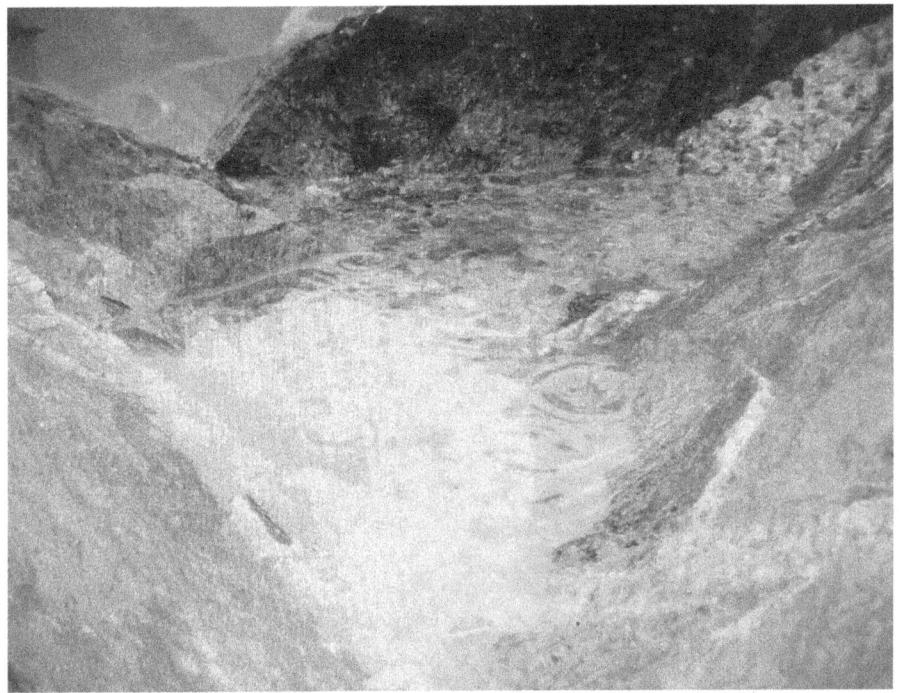

Figure 1
Asbestos Soup

This photo presents a view of pure, natural chrysotile eroded from exposed seams by rainwater and accumulated into a small, soupy puddle. The "asbestos soup" was located on top of a concave portion of a chrysotile-bearing boulder at an asbestos mine in the Town of Asbestos, Quebec, Canada (mine in background).

Photo credit: By Asbestorama, Flickr

Figure 2
Asbestos Boulder at Mine

This photo is a partial view of a boulder with crisscrossing 1-inch veins of fibrous chrysotile in dark grey-green host matrix rock, located at a chrysotile asbestos mine in the town of Asbestos, Quebec in Canada. The boulder was placed for observation at a benched area within the mine's southeastern upper boundary along the pit's rim. Partial views of the pit's rim and large tailings piles can be seen in background.

Evidence of chrysotile material is everywhere inside the mine area: chrysotile gravel, chrysotile erosion & runoff, chrysotile mud, chrysotile tailings, chrysotile dust, etc. At the time of this photo, this mine in Asbestos, Quebec was reported as North America's last full-time operating asbestos mine.

Photo credit: By Asbestorama, Flickr

3.0 Canadian federal asbestos controls

The Canadian federal government plays a role in the control of asbestos risks through restrictions on the use of asbestos in certain products and applications; the mandatory labeling of asbestos-containing products (in amounts greater than 0.1% by weight); limits on environmental releases from asbestos mining and milling operations; the collection of data on annual releases, discharges, and asbestos disposal; and minimum standards for workplace exposures.

As a result of public concern about the risks to health and safety associated with asbestos mining and milling operations in Canada, in 1977 the federal government passed regulations to limit asbestos emissions to air under the federal *Clean Air Act (CAA)*.[13] In 1990 these asbestos regulations were updated when the *CAA* was repealed and the *CEPA* was enacted. *CEPA* provides the federal government with authority to regulate toxic substances and enables Environment Canada to place prohibitions on the production, emission, import, and export of many toxic substances through regulations issued under the act.[14]

The Asbestos Mines and Mills Release Regulations (SOR/90-341) state that no more than two asbestos fibers per normal cubic centimeter (2.0 f/cc) may be released into the ambient air from an asbestos mine or mill during (1) crushing, drying, or milling operations; (2) dry rock storage; or (3) primary dry-drilling operations in an open pit. Additional provisions address source testing and measurement methods, releases during breakdowns or malfunctions, and the submission of information, reports, and/or samples to Environment Canada.

While there are limits on concentrations (per cubic centimeter during a certain specified period of time) that can be discharged by a mining or milling plant, there is no overall limit on the total amount of asbestos that an operation may discharge.

How are asbestos discharges from manufacturing plants tracked?

Asbestos is a regulated substance under the National Pollutant Release Inventory (NPRI) established under *CEPA*. Designated industries are required to report on their use and discharge of asbestos in its friable form. Facilities are required to submit an annual NPRI report if they manufactured, processed, or otherwise used ten tons or more of friable asbestos at the facility where employees (including contractors) worked twenty thousand hours or more in a year.[15]

In 2008 over 8,700 facilities reported on the release, discharge, or disposal of 347 substances or families of substances to NPRI; of these, sixty-seven facilities across Canada and thirty in Ontario reported use of asbestos in excess of the ten-ton threshold reporting limit. Across Canada a total of 21,721 tons of asbestos was disposed of onsite by these facilities and 4,687 tons were shipped offsite for disposal. A total of 685 tons of friable asbestos was also "released" to land (a category that includes spills, leaks, and other uncontrolled releases of pollutants, but does not include disposal methods such as landfilling) during 2008. Appendix 5 contains a summary of the amounts of asbestos disposed of onsite and offsite by NPRI-listed facilities located in Ontario. The public can search the NPRI database to access specific facility-reported information on pollutant releases and transfers from the NPRI website at www.ec.gc.ca/inrp-npri/.

Ontario also requires the monitoring and reporting of pollutant releases under O. Reg. 127/01, made under the *EPA*.[16] However effective February 20, 2008, the MOE amended O. Reg. 127/01 to harmonize the province's air emissions reporting system with that of the federal government's NPRI program and reduce the compliance burden on Ontario facilities. Amendments were made to the MOE's "Step by Step Guideline for Emission Calculation, Record Keeping and Reporting for Airborne

Contaminant Discharge"[17] and to O. Reg. 127/01 to delist all substances except for acetone. Whether reporting emissions under O. Reg. 127/01 or the NPRI program, Ontario-based facilities will continue to use the national web-based reporting system called OWNERS (the One Window to National Environmental Reporting System).[18]

Labeling of products containing asbestos

The federal *HPA* requires suppliers of hazardous workplace materials—known as "controlled products"—to label containers and provide detailed hazard information through material safety data sheets (MSDS) as a condition of sale and importation. The Asbestos Products Regulations (SOR/2007-260), which updated and replaced the Hazardous Products (Crocidolite Asbestos) Regulations (SOR/89-440) under that act in 2007, are designed to:

- eliminate certain asbestos products (such as those used for modeling or sculpture, products that simulate ashes or embers, and any consumer product composed entirely of asbestos);
- restrict the use of crocidolite—one of the most dangerous forms of asbestos—to certain products (i.e., asbestos cement pipes, torque converters, diaphragms for chloralkali production, and acid and temperature resistant seals, gaskets, gland packings, and flexible couplings);
- require the labeling of crocidolite asbestos products and notification prior to the importation of crocidolite for the purposes of manufacturing; and
- impose conditional requirements on the use of other (non-crocidolite) asbestos products (for example a sprayed asbestos product must be encapsulated with a binder during application and must not become friable after drying).

In addition, according to the Ingredient Disclosure List (SOR/88-64) made under the *HPA*, any controlled product that contains asbestos, amosite asbestos, chrysotile asbestos, or crocidolite asbestos at concentrations greater than or equal to 0.1% (by weight) must include this information on the list of ingredients**Federal workplace standards**

The Canada Occupational Health and Safety Regulations (SOR/86-304), made under the *Canada Labour Code*, sets a workplace exposure limit for airborne chrysotile asbestos of 1 f/cc (which is ten times the Ontario limit). The regulations reference the Threshold Limit Values (TLV) and Biological Exposure Indices recommended by the American Conference of Governmental Industrial Hygienists (ACGIH) for all other chemical agents, with the exception of grain dust and airborne chrysotile asbestos. The ACGIH guidelines recommend a TLV for asbestos (all forms) of 0.1 f/cc; the value applies to fibers longer than 5 microns, with an aspect ratio of equal than/greater than 3:1, as determined by the membrane filter method at 400–450 times magnification (4 mm objective), using phase-contrast illumination.

4.0 Ontario's environmental controls on asbestos

A sbestos waste is not listed as a "hazardous waste" in RRO 1990, Reg. 347 (General—Waste Management) under the *EPA*. However a number of provisions in section 17 of the regulation apply specifically to the management of asbestos wastes. The overall objective of these provisions is summed up by the general prohibition set out in subsection 17(16), which states that every person involved in the transportation, handling, or management of asbestos waste "shall take all precautions necessary to prevent asbestos waste from becoming airborne."[19]

Regulation 347 establishes rules for the management of asbestos wastes based on the amount of asbestos waste and the source of asbestos waste, i.e., domestic waste, commercial waste, non-hazardous industrial waste, and hazardous waste.

Most asbestos wastes are generated when insulation or fireproofing materials are removed from equipment or buildings. The MOE has developed a Regulatory framework and established policies to address the safe handling and disposal of these "bulk" wastes. [20] The MOE allows bulk asbestos wastes to be transported to landfill sites and transfer stations, subject to compliance with a number of strict rules and policies (as outlined below and described in more detail in Appendix 4).

Regulation 347 permits the disposal of small amounts of asbestos waste in any landfill site approved for the disposal of municipal waste. Regulation

347 defines both "commercial waste" and "domestic waste" as including asbestos waste. These definitions appear intended to facilitate disposal of commercial and domestic products that contain "trivial" amounts of asbestos in landfills that are licensed to accept solid, non-hazardous waste.

Section 1 of Regulation 347 further states that "non-hazardous solid industrial waste" means "industrial waste that is not liquid industrial waste and is not hazardous waste *and includes asbestos waste*" [emphasis added]. Section 1 goes on to specify that "asbestos waste" means "solid or liquid waste that results from the removal of asbestos-containing construction or insulation materials or the manufacture of asbestos-containing products and contains asbestos in more than a trivial amount or proportion."

Neither the *EPA* nor Regulation 347 defines "trivial", but the MOE advised the ECO in early 2008 that ministry staff uses the MOL's definition of asbestos-containing material to define a trivial amount of asbestos waste. Under O. Reg. 278/05 (Designated Substance—Asbestos on Construction Projects and in Buildings and Repair Operations) made under the *OHSA,* the MOL requires special handling of asbestos-containing material that contain 0.5 percent or more asbestos by dry weight.[21]

According to ss.17(1) of Regulation 347, generators and transporters of bulk (more than a trivial amount) asbestos waste are required to notify landfill and transfer station operators before the waste is delivered to their sites so that the operators may agree to accept it and to schedule the anticipated time of the waste's arrival.

Determinations of trivial amounts of asbestos waste are made by the landfill and transfer station operators at the time the wastes arrive at the site. The MOE also notes that "there is written internal guidance for MOE staff, but none formally exists for the regulated community at this time. MOE staff provides direction to the regulated community on determining trivial amounts either verbally or in writing if requested." However the MOE's guidance is not legally binding on landfill operators and other regulated persons subject to Regulation 347.

In addition to allowing asbestos disposal in regular landfill sites, s.17 of Regulation 347 imposes standards for waste handling, packaging, transportation, vehicles, and disposal sites related to asbestos. Operators are required to obtain a Certificate of Approval (C of A) for a waste management system under s. 27 of the *EPA* before they can transport any waste.

Under s. 17 of Regulation 347, non-trivial quantities of asbestos waste transported to a waste disposal site must be shipped in a rigid, impermeable, sealed container of sufficient strength to accommodate the weight and nature of the waste, or it must be shipped in bulk by a hauler with an approved C of A that specifically authorizes the transportation of bulk asbestos waste.

Subsection 17(10) stipulates that asbestos waste may be deposited only at locations in a landfill that "have been adapted for the purpose of receiving asbestos waste or are otherwise suitable for that purpose" and ss. 17(11) states that the waste may be deposited at a landfill site only while the depositing is supervised by the operator of the site or the person's designate. Subsection 17(12) requires that deposited asbestos waste must be covered by at least 125 centimeters of solid waste or cover material and "direct contact with compaction equipment or other equipment operating on the site should be avoided."

Guidelines for handling asbestos waste

The MOE has also developed two guidelines that relate to the handling of asbestos waste. Guideline C-6 (titled "Handling, Transportation and Disposal of Asbestos Waste in Bulk") provides basic standards for the assessment of vehicles, equipment, and procedures used for the collection, transportation, and disposal of asbestos waste in bulk. The guideline—last updated in 1994—is "intended for use by operators of bulk asbestos waste handling and transportation systems, and by Ministry staff members during their review and assessment of C of A applications for bulk asbestos waste systems and during monitoring." The guideline also states that asbestos waste should be "transported directly to a landfill site at which the operator has been informed in advance of the quantity of the waste and the approximate time of arrival."

Procedure C-10 (titled "Removal Procedures at Sites Containing Substantial Quantities of Asbestos Waste") is intended to protect the environment during the excavation and removal of asbestos waste from landfill sites, tailings disposal areas, industrial properties, or other sites prior to their redevelopment or for other purposes. Last updated in 1994, the procedure applies to sites containing substantial quantities of asbestos waste.

Procedure C-10 recommends that all employees working on the operations "shall be protected by the use of respirators and clothing as necessary or as directed" by the consultant or MOL staff, and stipulates that "the requirements of the *Occupational Health and Safety Act* and its regulations shall be adhered to by all personnel involved in the operations."

Enforcement

In cases where contractors or waste operators fail to comply with provisions of Regulation 347, the MOE has prosecuted them. For example in the fall of 2002, a London-based contractor was awarded a demolition contract requiring him to remove and dispose of asbestos waste at a long-term care facility for senior citizens, in accordance with Regulation 347.[22] However the contractor bagged some of the asbestos waste and transported it to asbestos waste bins owned by a disposal company in London without notifying that company. An investigation by the MOE's Investigation and Enforcement Branch confirmed that a quantity of asbestos waste was transported without a C of A for a waste management system contrary to ss. 27(1) of the *EPA* and the contractor was charged. In June 2005, the contractor was fined $45,000 for transporting asbestos waste without a C of A.

In the past, the MOE has attempted to apply section 17 of Regulation 347 to the handling of asbestos insulation within the building from which the waste was being removed.[23] As one commentator has noted, the better view is that the *OHSA* provides "a complete code for the regulation of indoor asbestos" and that this regulation only applies after asbestos is removed from the building[24] because section 1 of the *EPA* defines "air" as outdoor air.

Asbestos waste generated by field operations (including remote sites operated by power or pipeline networks, equipment service contractors, and mobile health care providers) can be transferred to a local waste transfer facility without notice to the MOE.

Current status of asbestos landfilling by contractors and haulers

Each year thousands of tons of waste containing asbestos generated by construction and renovation work in Ontario are disposed of at landfills serving Ontario residents, municipalities, and companies. At present most municipal and private landfill and transfer station operators charge an additional fee (from $20 to more than $400/ton) to handle and/or safely dispose of asbestos waste and have developed special policies to be notified in advance of delivery.[25] For example, the City of London, Ontario, charges a lump sum of $300 plus $75/ton for the landfill disposal of asbestos waste. Effective April 1, 2010, the City of Ottawa charges a tipping fee of $410/ton (or a flat rate of $100 if under 255 kg) for the dumping of asbestos at its Trail Waste Facility. The City of Brantford charges $120/ton for the disposal of asbestos at its Mohawk Street Sanitary Landfill Site.

To maintain access to its Michigan landfill site, the City of Toronto's municipal code prohibits the receipt at its transfer stations of asbestos waste, banned from Michigan landfills. The by-law came into effect on October 1, 2004, and enforcement began immediately. Asbestos waste is not collected curbside or through any City of Toronto programs. Residents are directed to make arrangements with a private sector company that specializes in disposing of this type of waste.

There may be certain landfills in Ontario that accept more bulk asbestos waste or used products containing asbestos and a different approach is warranted in those cases. Moreover it is conceivable that some shipments of construction and demolition waste contain various quantities of asbestos waste that were released during renovations or in the demolition of buildings constructed in the past century.[26] In June 2006, the ECO received an application for review proposing that products containing small amounts of asbestos should not be disposed in landfills regulated and designed to accept non-hazardous solid waste.[27]

How does the MOE Regulate asbestos in Ontario's ambient air?

Low levels of asbestos can be found in the outdoor air in most communities because of its widespread use in various products sold and distributed in the past century. Most experts agree that these levels present little overall risk to most people's health.[28] For example ten fibers are usually present in a cubic meter (fibers/m³) of outdoor air in rural areas in the United States.[29] (A cubic meter is about the amount of air that an average-sized adult breathes in one hour.)[30]

Levels of asbestos found in cities tend to be higher than those in rural areas—often about ten times higher.[31] For example asbestos has been reported to be present at 3 x 10^{-6} to 3 x 10^{-4} fibers/ml or 3 to 300 fibers per cubic meter (0.1 to 10 ng/m^3) in many urban areas in Ontario.[32] According to a lengthy toxicology study prepared for the City of Toronto in 2002, the outdoor levels of asbestos in some urban areas in Ontario can range up to 3 x 10^{-3} fibers/ml or 3,000 fibers per cubic meter (or 100 ng/m^3).[33]

Studies in the United States suggest that levels of asbestos close to an asbestos mine or factory may reach 10,000 fibers/m^3 or higher.[34] Levels could also be elevated near waste sites where asbestos wastes are not properly covered or stored to protect them from animals or wind erosion, or at construction sites where older buildings that contain asbestos products are being renovated or torn down.

The MOE sets environmental quality standards "to protect human and ecosystem health, prevent damage such as soiling and corrosion to the physical environment."[35] According to the MOE, standards are used by ministry staff and management to determine compliance with Ontario's environmental regulations and to define the legal limits for discharges to air and water in Certificates of Approval, control orders, and program approvals issued under the *EPA* and the *Ontario Water Resources Act (OWRA)*.[36]

In 2005 the Ontario government passed O. Reg. 419/05 to update the regulatory framework for safeguarding local air quality and also amended its ambient air quality criteria (AAQC) and point of impingement (POI) guidelines.[37] The amendments included the development of contaminant-specific AAQCs protective of human and environmental health. These criteria are effects-based and were developed to be protective of the most sensitive ecological receptors or human populations (such as children and the elderly) and do not consider technological or economic issues.

As part of its air standards updating process related to O. Reg. 419/05, the MOE released a summary of the new POI guidelines and revised AAQCs. Under O. Reg. 419/05, an MOE director can issue notices and impose certain notification requirements on dischargers. Exceeding a POI guideline or AAQC may cause adverse effects and could trigger the issuance of a director's notice. With respect to asbestos, the 2005 criterion for ambient air is no more than 0.04 asbestos fibers of length greater than 5 µm per cubic centimeter of air.[38] The POI guideline is 5 µg per cubic meter of air in a thirty-minute period.

There may be some ongoing confusion about the differing air standards promulgated under the province's environmental and the occupational health and safety regulatory regimes. The MOE's AAQC of 0.04 fibers per cubic centimeter (f/cc) has been set to protect the most vulnerable members of society over a lifetime of exposure. The MOL's occupational exposure limit of 0.1 f/cc has been set to protect a healthy adult on the worksite eight hours a day, forty hours a week, and for a working lifetime without adverse effects.

5.0 Ontario's Occupational Health & Safety controls on asbestos

The *OHSA* is the main law governing workplace health and safety in Ontario. The purpose of the *OHSA* is to protect workers against health and safety hazards in the workplace. It sets out the rights and duties of all parties in the workplace, establishes procedures for dealing with hazards, and provides for the enforcement of the law where compliance has not been adhered to voluntarily.

The *OHSA* is based on the principle of an internal responsibility system where workplace parties—employers, workers, supervisors, constructors and licensees, suppliers, owners, and the directors and officers of a corporation—identify, develop, and implement solutions to workplace health and safety issues.

The *OHSA* also gives the Ontario government broad power to design regulations, setting out in detail how some duties of various parties are to be carried out. Moreover the general provision in *OHSA* requires employers to "take every precaution reasonable in the circumstances for the protection of a worker." Thus the MOL may cite provisions in any of these regulations as a "reasonable precaution" and cause them to be enforced by a written order. For example MOL inspectors have in numerous cases invoked RRO 1990, Regulation 692 (Regulation for Industrial Establishments) to control workplace hazards.

Several regulations under the *OHSA* provide clear and detailed requirements for the management of asbestos in buildings and during construction and renovation. In addition occupational exposure limits have been set for asbestos under the Control of Exposure to Biological or Chemical Agents Regulation (RRO 1990, Reg. 833).

Consolidated Designated Substances Regulation

The *OHSA* allows a toxic substance to be "designated", and its use in the workplace to be either strictly controlled or banned. According to the MOL, designation is reserved for particularly hazardous substances.

The MOL takes a slightly different approach to designated substances (such as asbestos) than it does to most other workplace chemical, mineral, and biological agents. [39]For most workplace agents, the legislation imposes a general duty on employers to protect worker health, undertake training, provide personal protective equipment, and so on, and then sets workplace limits on permissible exposures. It is largely up to the employer to determine how to conform to that standard. However when it comes to the riskiest agents—the aforementioned designated substances—the province becomes more prescriptive, dictating in some detail the steps that must be followed to ensure a safe workplace.

In 1982 the Minister of Labour designated asbestos a regulated substance under *OHSA* with the passage of O. Reg. 570/82, Designated Substance—Asbestos. O. Reg. 570/82 (which was subsequently consolidated in 1992 as RRO 1990, Reg. 837). This was one of a series of twelve designated substances regulations and addressed the use of asbestos in the "fixed place" processes of mining, manufacturing, and assembling goods or products. The other eleven designated substances regulations covered the use of asbestos in construction projects and in buildings and repair operations, as well as acrylonitrile, arsenic, benzene, coke oven emissions, ethylene oxide, isocyanates, lead, mercury, silica, and vinyl chloride.

In June 2007, two Ontario companies were fined more than $175,000 under Regulation 837 after failing to provide asbestos removal workers with appropriate personal protective equipment.

On December 17, 2009, a new *OHSA* regulation was filed with the Registrar of Regulations, consolidating eleven of the twelve stand-alone designated substance regulations into a single regulation. This regulation, O. Reg. 490/09 (Designated Substances), came into effect on July 1, 2010. This regulation repealed RRO 1990, Reg. 837; however, O. Reg. 278/05 (Asbestos on Construction Projects and in Buildings and Repair Operations) was not consolidated with the others in O. Reg. 490/09 and remains separate.

O. Reg. 490/09 applies (with respect to asbestos) to the mining, crushing, grinding, or sifting of asbestos, and the processing, adaptation, or use of asbestos in the manufacture or assembling of goods or products. In addition the regulation covers the repair, alteration, or maintenance of machinery, equipment, aircraft, ships, locomotives, railway cars, and vehicles (as well as work on a building that is necessarily incidental to the repair, alteration, or maintenance of machinery or equipment) if an employer had implemented an asbestos control program in accordance with the regulations prior to December 16, 1985, and has continued to maintain the measures and procedures of that program. If that is not the case, then O. Reg. 278/05 applies.

Similar to Regulation 837, O. Reg. 490/09 prescribes occupational exposure limits (OEL) to restrict worker exposure to asbestos and prescribes codes for respiratory equipment, medical surveillance, and the measurement of airborne fibers.

Under section 16(2) of O. Reg. 490/09, every employer must take "all necessary measures and procedures by means of engineering controls, work practices and hygiene facilities and practices" to ensure that a worker's airborne exposure to asbestos is reduced to "the lowest practical level" and, in any event, does not exceed 0.1 fibers per cubic centimeter. Subject to the exceptions set forth in section 18 of the regulation, an employer must comply with this section without requiring a worker to wear and use respiratory equipment. An employer can provide respiratory equipment if it is otherwise impossible to meet the standard because: 1) an emergency exists; 2) the measures necessary to control exposures do not exist, are not available, or are not reasonable or practical for the length of time necessary for protection or the frequency of exposure; 3) the nature of the process, operation or work requires special equipment; or 4) the standards are not likely to be effective because of a temporary breakdown of equipment.

Asbestos on construction projects and in buildings and repair operations

O. Reg. 278/05 (Designated Substance—Asbestos on Construction Projects and in Buildings and Repair Operations) outlines the requirements for the management of asbestos in buildings and during construction and renovation. A facility owner must comply with all parts of the regulation and the act if the building contains asbestos. O. Reg. 278/05 differs from the approach in O. Reg. 490/09 in that it neither sets an OEL nor requires monitoring. Instead O. Reg. 278/05 prescribes safe work procedures (e.g., how to remove asbestos material) and outlines measures to control worker exposure, such as the isolation of work areas and the use of air-purifying respirators and prescribes conditions which contravene the regulations.[40]

An important requirement of O. Reg. 278/05 is an Owner's Asbestos Report which must be prepared when an owner proposes construction or repair projects in buildings whether

asbestos-containing material is or is not present.[41] (Asbestos-containing material is defined as containing 0.5% or more asbestos.) If asbestos is present, the report must: (1) contain drawings, plans, or specifications showing the location of the asbestos; (2) for each location, state the condition of the asbestos and whether the material is friable or non-friable; and (3) identify the type of asbestos (e.g., chrysotile, crocidolite, tremolite, etc.) if the material is sprayed on.

If the composition of material encountered during the course of work is unknown, the owner can have it tested to determine its content. Otherwise the work must be done as if the material contains asbestos—and a type of asbestos other than chrysotile, if the material is sprayed on. If it is determined that asbestos-containing material is present ahead of time, the owner's asbestos report must state this. The owner must provide the asbestos report to all contractors bidding on the job. The contractor must provide the report to all subcontractors and workers.

Exemptions for homeowners and small residential building owners

Exemptions for homeowners and small residential building owners from O. Reg. 278/05 are set out in subsections 2(3) and 2(4). The regulation does not apply: (1) to the owner of a private home that is occupied by the owner or the owner's family; and (2) to the owner of a residential building that contains no more than four units, one of which is occupied by the registered owner or family of the registered owner. This means that small asbestos removal projects carried out by a homeowner are not subject to O. Reg. 278/05. However the regulation does apply to contractors, employers, and workers engaged in private construction projects and repair or maintenance of such buildings.

In the event that a contractor is to be hired, section 30 of the *OHSA* requires homeowners (and any owner of any project site) to prepare a list of all designated substances (including asbestos) onsite and include this list with tendering information. The list must go to the contractor, and the contractor must give it to subcontractors and workers before the contract for work is finalized.

The specific requirements have been outlined in a guide published by the MOL in November 2007 and are available on its website at: www. labour.gov.on.ca/english/hs/pdf/asbestos_guide.pdf

Occupational exposure limits for asbestos

Ontario has added a new OEL for asbestos in its amended Control of Exposure to Biological or Chemical Agents Regulation (RRO 1990, Reg. 833) under the *OHSA*. The revised Table of Ontario Occupational Exposure Limits (Table 1 in the Regulation), which took effect July 1, 2010, sets a time-weighted average (TWA) OEL for asbestos (all forms) of 0.1 fibers per cubic centimeter, as well as the same TWA for each of the major individual forms of asbestos (i.e., actinolite, amosite, anthophyllite, chrysotile, crocidolite, and tremolite). These new limits apply specifically to the most dangerous asbestos fibers, long and thin ("longer than 5 μm in length and less than 3 μm in width and that have a length to width ratio not less than 3:1").

The OEL for asbestos does *not* apply to construction projects, to a workplace that is subject to O. Reg. 490/09 (Designated Substances), or to a workplace that is subject to O. Reg. 278/05 (Designated Substance—Asbestos on Construction Projects and in Buildings and Repair Operations). However it would apply to any other workplace.

6.0 Conclusion

The MOE and MOL have developed a fairly elaborate system for regulating the handling of asbestos waste generated by building repairs and site redevelopment, and there is evidence that these regulations are enforced and that the courts tend to impose large fines on contravenors. In addition the MOE's regulatory system is designed to promote safe disposal and handling of bulk quantities of products containing asbestos such as thermal insulation for pipes, brake linings, shingles, etc. The current regulatory system does not address the small quantities of asbestos wastes associated with manufactured products that are deposited in landfills on a regular basis.

About the Author

David S. McRobert is an environmental lawyer based in southern Ontario. Between October 1994 and June 2010, he was In-House Counsel and Senior Policy Advisor at the Environmental Commissioner of Ontario and was involved in the establishment of the office. David has a B.Sc. in Biology from Trent University (1980) and a Master's degree in Environmental Studies (MES) from York University (1984). He graduated with an LL.B. degree from Osgoode Hall Law School (1987) and was admitted to the Ontario Bar in 1990.

Before joining the ECO, David was a senior policy advisor in the Waste Reduction Office in the Ontario Ministry of the Environment. From 1989 to 1991, he coordinated research and advocacy on waste management and global warming at Pollution Probe. He has also worked for the Workplace Health and Safety Agency in Toronto, the Ontario Round Table on Environment and Economy, the Ministry of Labour, and the Ministry of the Attorney General.

David has published numerous articles and reports on a range of environmental issues. In the past two decades, he has prepared a number of reports, articles, and conference papers on a range of environmental subjects, including public participation and government accountability for environmental decision-making. Between 1991 and 2009, he taught

courses on environmental law and policy to undergraduate students in the
Faculty of Environmental Studies at York University and the University of
Toronto.

www.davidmcrobert.ca

Appendix 1

Tips for homeowners on the management of asbestos waste

The following information has been provided for homeowners and tenants to assist in the assessment, containment/removal, handling, transportation, and disposal of asbestos waste. While homeowners are not prohibited from undertaking asbestos removal and other potentially dangerous remediation work, they are strongly encouraged to seek out expert advice in order to verify the presence (and type) of asbestos present in their homes and to learn how to minimize the risks incurred by them and their families, tenants, and neighbors if they attempt to undertake the work themselves. It is also important to ensure that any contractor they hire holds the requisite license (as the homeowner may be held liable in the event of a workplace incident). In addition there is evidence that asbestos was a component of some insulation products that were installed in Ontario homes and buildings between the late 1950s and the 1970s.[42]

Decisions to remove asbestos waste or asbestos-containing products from residential buildings and how to conduct the removal should be carefully considered by home and building owners before proceeding.

To protect health and safety, environmental remediation contractors companies rely on high efficiency particulate air (HEPA) machines and

portable air scrubbers for HEPA filtration and negative pressure during asbestos abatement. Further information about proper equipment and techniques is available in publications available through the MOL's website at
www.labour.gov.on.ca/english/hs/pdf/asbestos_guide.pdf

As noted above, in some cases, it may be advisable to leave certain materials—such as insulation products manufactured with an asbestos component—in place. In other cases, deteriorating or friable asbestos should be removed. In every case, it is advisable to obtain the expert opinion of a licensed asbestos removal contractor. There are many specialized waste management companies and environmental remediation contractors who are experts in handling and removing asbestos.

Once asbestos or waste material containing asbestos is removed from a residential building, the waste generator must determine if the waste is subject to RRO 1990, Reg. 347 or if the amount is trivial and Regulation 347 does not apply.[43] As noted above, material that contains 0.5 percent or more asbestos by dry weight is non-trivial and is subject to MOE regulation. In practical terms, this means that very small amounts of asbestos waste can trigger application of Regulation 347. In such cases, waste asbestos must be transported and managed according to the *EPA*, Regulation 347, applicable certificates of approval, and local landfill rules. The MOE does not currently have a publication available setting out its requirements, but contractors must follow the requirements in O. Reg. 278/05.[44]

Homeowners and contractors also should keep in mind that landfill and transfer station operators must be notified by the generators of asbestos waste of delivery of the waste material so that the operators may agree to accept it and obtain an anticipated time of arrival as required by ss. 17(1) of Regulation 347. Most municipal landfill operators charge an additional fee (ranging from $20 to $300 per ton) to handle and safely dispose of asbestos waste.[45]

As a general rule, Regulation 347 is not directed at non-friable materials (such as brake linings, tiles, or woven cloth). Asbestos that is tightly bound within a solid matrix so that it is not easily crumbled by hand is considered non-friable; such material is not usually a significant risk in a home setting when it is handled properly. The MOE does not have a detailed list of products containing asbestos, but advises that any person, contractor, or company seeking to dispose of material that contains 0.5 percent or more asbestos by dry weight needs to follow the special handling requirements in section 17 of Regulation 347.[46]

Some experts suggest that you inquire of your local municipality or waste hauler about whether it is acceptable to deposit asbestos products that are tightly bound within a solid matrix at the curb for pickup with your domestic waste. However this report does not advocate this approach to disposal because of the risk to municipal waste workers and local residents in your community.

In those cases when you decide to hire a contractor to undertake work involving asbestos, make sure that the contractor has all the appropriate tools, training, licensing, and certification necessary to comply with the law and to protect you from unnecessary exposure to asbestos fibers. Do-it-yourself asbestos removal could prove very costly. You could compromise the health of your family, leading to disability or disease, and any short-term savings could seem trivial in hindsight.

Appendix 2

Health risks related to asbestos exposure

Occupational exposure to airborne respirable asbestos fibers can lead to the development of a number of diseases and medical conditions, including asbestosis, malignant mesothelioma, lung cancer and other forms of cancer, pleural plaques, asbestos bodies, and warts. The length, diameter, and chemical composition of the asbestos fibers, as well as the duration of exposure and individual susceptibility, all have an impact on subsequent health effects.

Asbestosis

Asbestosis is found in workers and the general public who have been exposed to relatively high levels of asbestos over a long period of time. Asbestosis occurs when asbestos fibers become lodged in the lungs, irritating the lung tissues and inflaming the organ's small air tubes and sacs.[47] As the inflammation heals, permanent scar tissue (fibrosis) develops. The scarring causes shortness of breath which grows worse over time—even after exposure ceases. Eventually it may become nearly impossible for the victim to inhale enough air; the most common cause of death is cardiac arrest caused by increased heart strain. The disease is much less likely to occur if proper precautions are taken. There is no known cure for asbestosis. The Workplace Safety and Insurance Board of Ontario (WSIB), which compensates workers and their families for injuries and deaths associated with workplace hazards, allows claims for asbestosis when it can be demonstrated that a worker was exposed to asbestos dust for at least two years.[48]

Malignant mesothelioma

Malignant mesothelioma is a rare form of cancer that is almost always caused by exposure to asbestos. While cumulative exposures to limits above the current workplace standards increase the risk of developing mesothelioma, studies show that it may result from relatively minimal exposure to certain kinds of asbestos. Mesothelioma is rarely associated with chrysotile asbestos exposure alone; a history of exposure to amphibole (usually crocidolite) or amphibole-chrysotile mixtures is common. This cancer occurs in the pleura (the lining of the chest) or the peritoneum (the lining of the abdomen). In its early stages, symptoms include shortness of breath or pain in the chest or abdomen. Mesothelioma occurs in only one in every hundred thousand people not exposed to asbestos. However one study found that ten of the 124 deaths of asbestos insulation workers could be attributed to mesothelioma.[49] There is no cure for this disease. Most of the victims die within one or two years of diagnosis.[50]

Lung cancer

Studies show that lung cancer is more common in people exposed to asbestos than in individuals who have not been exposed. Early symptoms include coughing, chest pain, and coughing up blood. Smoking greatly increases the risk of developing lung cancer from exposure to asbestos. Some studies suggest that a smoker who is heavily exposed to asbestos is thirty to ninety times more likely to develop lung cancer than a non-smoker.[51]

The U.S. Environmental Protection Agency has estimated the inhalation cancer potency of asbestos to be 0.23 per fiber per milliliter (fiber/ml).[52] This corresponds to a lifetime cancer risk of one in a million if individuals are exposed to asbestos at an air level of 4×10^{-6} fiber/ml over a lifetime[53] (or about 0.1 nanograms/m^3).

As with asbestosis, proper precautions can help reduce the risk of developing asbestos-related lung cancer. If the cancer is detected early, surgical treatment is often an option (to remove cancerous tissue).

Other cancers

Some studies suggest that exposure to asbestos also results in cancers of the esophagus, stomach, colon, rectum, and gastrointestinal tract. It has been suggested that these diseases may be caused when a victim swallows some of the longer asbestos fibers that become lodged in the upper air passages. The fibers are then carried to the throat in mucus and through the rest of the digestive tract.

Other effects

A number of less serious medical conditions have been associated with asbestos exposure, including pleural plaques (scarring of the pleural surface), asbestos bodies, and warts. For decades most have been thought to be harmless by medical professionals but they may serve as an indicator of asbestos exposure.

Appendix 3

How the EBR applies to asbestos handling and asbestos risks

The Ontario *Environmental Bill of Rights(EBR)* applies to asbestos handling and waste disposal operations in several ways. It affords the public the right to comment on certain proposals, appeal some decisions, and submit applications for review and investigation. Those laws, ministries, and instruments subject to the public notification and comment provisions under the *EBR* are set forth in O. Reg. 73/94 and O. Reg. 681/94 and updated from time to time as deemed necessary.

Since the *EBR* came into force in 1994, dozens of Ontario residents have contacted the ECO to request information on how to handle asbestos or to ask for assistance in locating information about current Ontario laws and policies on asbestos handling and risks to human health.

The opportunity to comment

When a ministry puts a proposal on the Environmental Registry website, residents and non-residents of Ontario have an opportunity to provide input before the ministry makes a final decision. Comments must be submitted in writing, by deadline, to the contact person listed on the notice. The comment must reference the *EBR* Registry number.

Acts, Regulations and policies

The general public (including non-residents of Ontario) also has the right to comment on proposals for new or amended acts, regulations, or policies related to the MOE's work regulating asbestos handling and disposal and the health risks from airborne asbestos contaminants. For example in 2005 the MOE passed O. Reg. 419/05 to update the regulatory framework for local air quality and also amended its AAQC guidelines (including those for asbestos), and the public was invited to comment. Similar types of initiatives could be subject to Environmental Registry notices in the future.

Instruments

The public may also comment on some licenses, permits, C of As, and other decisions issued under the *EPA*. The public comment period is usually thirty days. The instruments may involve waste sites where disposal of bulk asbestos wastes is permitted, or the approval of machines and equipment that are involved in processing of asbestos-containing material or wastes. C of As for haulers of wastes (including asbestos wastes) are not prescribed instruments under the *EBR* and are not posted on the Registry for comment.

The opportunity to request leave to appeal an approval

The *EBR* provides Ontario residents with the right to seek leave (or permission) to appeal some ministry decisions on instruments, such as approvals and licenses. The *EBR* sets out a two-step process: (1) requesting leave to appeal is the first step; (2) if leave is granted, the appeal or hearing may proceed. Operations cannot proceed until the appeal is decided, unless the tribunal agrees to waive this restriction at the request of the proponent.

Generally the public has fifteen calendar days to submit a request after a ministry gives notice of a decision on the Registry. Application for leave to appeal is made to the appropriate appeal body, with notice to the ECO and the ministry issuing the approval. Appealing a ministry decision on an instrument takes time, money, and expertise, and you may wish to hire a lawyer. See the ECO publication *"EBR and You"* for more general information on leave to appeal, or contact the appropriate appeal body for information about its procedures.

MOE decisions on C of As for waste site approvals and for air discharges from specific operations are subject to leave to appeal. The Environmental Review Tribunal handles appeals under MOE legislation. These procedures provide a mechanism to raise concerns about the adequacy of conditions of approval related to asbestos risks.

The opportunity to request a review or investigation

Reviews and investigations are two important tools under the *EBR*. For both processes, requests are made to the appropriate ministry by submitting an application to the Environmental Commissioner. The Office of the ECO acts as a clearing house for Applications for Review and Investigation by forwarding applications to the appropriate ministry and reviewing how the ministry responds to the application.

Applications for Review—changing old decisions or asking for new ones

Two persons who have lived in Ontario for a sufficient time to qualify, or residents or a combination of residents and corporate persons may ask to review an existing policy or a prescribed act, regulation, or instrument. For example if you were concerned about the need for better handling of waste at Ontario's landfill sites, you could ask for changes to the *EPA* or Regulation 347 to strengthen the legal or regulatory provisions regarding handling of asbestos wastes. Reviews of existing policies could also be requested for the handling of bulk asbestos wastes, as described above. Residents may also request a review of the need to establish a new policy, act, or regulation.

Applications for Investigation—if someone is breaking the law

If two residents believe that an act, regulation, or instrument prescribed under the *EBR* has been contravened, they may submit an Application for Investigation. An investigation could allege that any provision of the *EPA* or its regulations is being contravened. Ontario residents may also request an investigation by the MOE of alleged contraventions of any prescribed instruments under the *EPA* or *OWRA*. This would include alleged contraventions of C of As involving asbestos waste being improperly accepted and buried at a landfill site that is not licensed to accept asbestos waste.

Note that neither the MOL nor the *OHSA* are currently prescribed for *EBR* investigations or reviews. Thus it is presently not an option for Ontario residents to file an *EBR* application for review of asbestos handling standards under *OHSA* or an alleged contravention of asbestos handling in a workplace context. However it would be possible to request that the MOL and the *OHSA* be prescribed so that *EBR* investigations or reviews could be undertaken related to asbestos handling issues under *OHSA*.

For information on preparing applications under the *EBR*, please see our website at www.eco.on.ca and our publication "The *EBR* and You".

Right to Sue

The *EPA* and its regulations and instruments are subject to court actions under the "harm to a public resource" provisions of the *EBR*. A resident can sue if he or she thinks someone is breaking—or about to break—a law or regulation (such as Regulation 347) and harming a public resource (such as air, land, or water). The resident can usually sue only if the person previously received an unreasonable or untimely response to an Application for Investigation. If you want to sue, you are required to notify the ECO and the Attorney General of Ontario.

How to complain

All complaints respecting MOE-licensed operations should be directed to the MOE. Addresses and phone numbers for MOE Regional and district offices are available on the MOE's website: http://www.ene.gov.on.ca/envision/org/op.htm#Reg/Dist

Similarly all complaints respecting operations regulated under *OHSA* should be directed to the MOL. MOL contacts are listed on the MOL's website at:

http://www.labour.gov.on.ca/english/about/Reg_offices.html

Appendix 4

MOE's waste management procedures to prevent asbestos exposure

RRO 1990, Reg. 347—a regulation made under the *EPA*—permits the disposal of asbestos waste in any landfill site approved for the disposal of municipal waste. Section 1 of Regulation 347 states that "non-hazardous solid industrial waste" means industrial waste that is not liquid industrial waste and is not hazardous waste *and includes asbestos waste*. [Emphasis added]

Section 1 goes on to specify that "asbestos waste" means solid or liquid waste that results from the removal of asbestos-containing construction or insulation materials *or the manufacture of asbestos-containing products and contains asbestos in more than a trivial amount or proportion.* [Emphasis added]

Neither the *EPA* nor Regulation 347 define "trivial" but the Oxford English Dictionary defines trivial as "small and of little importance." Regulation 347 goes on to define both "commercial waste" and "domestic waste" as including asbestos waste. These definitions appear intended to facilitate disposal of commercial and domestic products that contain small amounts of asbestos in landfills that are licensed to accept solid non-hazardous waste.

In December 2007, the ECO asked the MOE to clarify how ministry staff and landfill and transfer station operators decide on what is a trivial amount of asbestos under Regulation 347 and whether there are any written guidelines. According to the MOE, ministry staff use the MOL's definition of asbestos-containing material: material that contains 0.5 per cent or more asbestos by dry weight in O. Reg. 278/05 made under the *OHSA*.[54] (See below for further discussion of this regulation.)

Landfill and transfer station operators are notified by the generators of asbestos waste that it is being transported so that the operators may agree to accept it and determine the anticipated time of arrival as per section 17(1) of Regulation 347. The determination of trivial amounts of asbestos waste is made by the generator to the landfill and transfer station operators. The MOE also notes that "there is written internal guidance for MOE staff, but none formally exists for the regulated community at this time. MOE staff provides direction to the regulated community on determining trivial amounts either verbally or in writing if requested."

In addition to allowing asbestos disposal in regular landfill sites, section 17 of Regulation 347 imposes standards for waste handling, packaging, transportation, vehicles, and disposal sites related to asbestos. Operators are required to obtain a C of A for a waste management system under s. 27 of the *EPA* before they can transport any waste.

Under s. 17 of Regulation 347, asbestos waste transported to a waste disposal site must be shipped in a rigid, impermeable, sealed container of sufficient strength to accommodate the weight and nature of the waste; or it must be shipped in bulk by a hauler with an approved C of A that specifically authorizes the transportation of bulk asbestos waste.

Subsection 17(10) stipulates that asbestos waste may be deposited only at locations in a landfill that "have been adapted for the purpose of receiving asbestos waste or are otherwise suitable for that purpose" and s. 17(11) goes on to state that the waste may be deposited at a landfilling site only as long as the depositing is being supervised by the operator of the site or the person's designate. Subsection 17(12) requires that deposited asbestos waste must be covered by at least 125 centimeters of solid waste or cover material and "direct contact with compaction equipment or other equipment operating on the site" should be avoided.

The MOE has also developed two guidelines that relate to the handling of asbestos waste. Guideline C-6—the Handling, Transportation and Disposal of Asbestos Waste in Bulk—provides basic standards for the assessment of vehicles, equipment, and procedures used for the collection, transportation, and disposal of asbestos waste in bulk. The guideline (last updated in 1994) is "intended for use by operators of bulk asbestos waste handling and transportation systems, and by Ministry staff during their review and assessment of C of A applications for bulk asbestos waste systems and during monitoring." The guideline also requires that asbestos waste should be "transported directly to a landfill site at which the operator has been informed in advance of the quantity of the waste and the approximate time of arrival."

Guideline C-6 also recommends that asbestos wastes generated when insulation or fireproofing materials are removed from equipment or buildings "be removed manually by scraping or brushing, or by using high pressure water." The MOE also advises that removal of asbestos by any of these methods "usually involves the use of water to lower the friability of asbestos and minimize the amount of fibers which may become airborne." In addition the MOE recommends that industrial vacuum loaders be used to collect asbestos removed using these methods.

Procedure C-10—Removal Procedures at Sites Containing Substantial Quantities of Asbestos Waste—is intended to protect the environment during the removal of asbestos waste from sites designated for redevelopment or other purposes. Last updated in 1994, the procedure applies to sites containing substantial quantities of asbestos waste.

Procedure C-10 recommends that all employees working on the operations "shall be protected by the use of respirators and clothing as necessary or as directed" by the consultant or MOL staff and stipulates that "the requirements of the *Occupational Health and Safety Act* and its regulations shall be adhered to by all personnel involved in the operations."

Procedure C-10 also suggests that ambient air at the worksite shall be "monitored according to ministry procedures" and the results evaluated against the MOE's primary criteria for ambient air is no more than "0.04 asbestos fibers of length greater than 5 μm per cubic centimeter of air" near sites containing large quantities of asbestos wastes. In addition samples shall be taken around the fence perimeter of the site. The number of samples is determined by the consultant and reviewed by MOE staff and results are evaluated in accordance with the MOE's primary criteria for asbestos in ambient air.

Procedure C-10 goes on to state that "should visible emissions occur onsite, remedial measures shall be taken" and the proponent's consultant "shall maintain a log of such events that records the time, duration, location, probable cause, and remedial measures applied" and make this log available to the Ministry. The log data is reviewed and compared with pertinent asbestos analytical data to ascertain if a relationship between the visible emission and asbestos fiber counts exists. In addition the MOE requires that post-removal air monitoring of the excavation site be conducted in a manner and frequency as determined by an MOE director.

Under Regulation 347 hazardous waste is defined as excluding asbestos waste as outlined above. In some cases, asbestos waste can become mixed with hazardous wastes and this may result in a classification of the mixture as hazardous. For hazardous wastes that are "subject wastes", section 18 of Regulation 347 requires waste generators to register with the MOE, to use manifests for tracking waste movements and to report to the director. The report is to be completed as directed in a guidance manual issued by the MOE. Subsequent changes to the type of subject wastes dealt with are to be sent to the director within fifteen days of the change, and records of the waste and how they are disposed of are to be maintained by the generator.

The requirements for manifests are outlined in sections 19–27 of Regulation 347. These sections require reporting and tracking waste movements whereby generators, carriers, waste disposal site operators, and waste-derived fuel site operators must submit copies of multi-part waste manifests to authorities and maintain copies for two years.

Proposals for reform in Ontario

In 1996 the MOE proposed to consolidate and revise existing waste management regulations as part of its Regulatory Reform Project. One goal of this review was to provide clear, consistent definitions, focus action on areas of highest environmental significance, increase waste diversion from landfills, improve compliance, and set clear, protective, environmental standards. In addition the proposed revisions to Regulation 347 were intended to take into consideration evolving waste management practices and incorporate administrative changes in support of an approvals process based on the level of environmental risk.

In 1998 the MOE tabled a detailed outline of its plans. Under the plan, amendments to Regulation 347 would have been introduced to clarify the definitions of asbestos and asbestos wastes to reflect new technologies and practices that were not available in the early 1980s when the MOE's first hazardous waste Regulations were developed and passed into law. The MOE claimed that updating the management requirements for asbestos waste would "enhance recycling opportunities, divert wastes from disposal, and offer certain cost savings." In 2002 the 1998 proposal was withdrawn by the MOE after the ECO requested an update on its status.

One change to Regulation 347 or to associated MOE policies and procedures worthy of further consideration is clarification of the quantities of asbestos waste that trigger application of the regulation. At present Regulation 347 stipulates that the asbestos waste must be in a quantity larger than a trivial amount, but there is no further detail provided in law or policy on what constitutes a trivial amount of asbestos. Regulations established by the province of British Columbia are more precise and indicate that "asbestos waste" is defined as a hazardous waste if it contains more than 1 percent (by weight) of friable asbestos fibers. It is noteworthy that, in response to a request for clarification made in December 2007, the MOE clarified that the MOL's definition of the amounts of asbestos triggering O. Reg. 278/05 (0.5 percent by weight) would apply.[55]

Appendix 5

Releases of asbestos by NPRI-listed facilities in Ontario, 2009

Facility	City	Onsite Disposal	Offsite Disposal
Lanxess Inc. – Lanxess West	Sarnia	0	66
Ethyl Canada Inc. – Corunna Site	Corunna	0	42
U.S. Steel Canada – Hamilton Works	Hamilton	0	36
Ontario Power Generation – Pickering Nuclear	Pickering	0	4.4
Imperial Oil – Sarnia Refinery Plant	Sarnia	0	123
Shell Canada – Sarnia Manufacturing Centre	Corunna	0	68
Durabla Canada	Belleville	0	0
Newalta Industrial Services Inc. – Taro Landfill 2	Stoney Creek	3,704	0
Sanofi Pasteur Limited – Connaught Campus	Toronto	0	55
TransAlta Energy – Sarnia Cogeneration Facility	Sarnia	0	13
Bruce Power Limited Partnership	Kincardine	0	38
Sault Ste. Marie Municipal Landfill	Sault Ste Marie	182	0
BFI Canada – Ridge Landfill	Blenheim	278	0
Imperial Oil – Sarnia Terminal	Sarnia	0	0

Waste Management Of Canada – Petrolia Landfill	Petrolia	2,802	0
Waste Services (CA) Inc. – Navan Landfill	Ottawa	282	0
Imperial Oil – Sarnia Chemical Plant	Sarnia	0	208
Newalta Corporation	Hamilton	0	2,793
Chemtura Canada CO/CIE	Elmira	0	1.3
Suncor Energy Products Inc. – Sarnia Refinery	Sarnia	0	24
Dow Chemical Canada Inc.	Sarnia	481	0
ArcelorMittal-Dofasco Inc.	Hamilton	0	7.4
Petro Canada – Mississauga Lubricant Center	Mississauga	0	25
Greater Toronto Airports Authority (GTAA) – Toronto Pearson International Airport	Toronto AMF	0	111
PPG Canada Inc. – Works 84, Owen Sound Flat Glass Plant	Owen Sound	0	0.003
Hotz Environmental Services Inc.	Hamilton	0	14
Waste Management Of Canada – Ottawa Landfill	Ottawa	225	0
Niagara Waste Systems Landfill Sites	Thorold	698	0
Imperial Oil – Sarnia Cogen	Sarnia	0	0
Int. Marine Salvage Inc. – Marine Recycling Corp.	Port Colborne	0	29
Total		8,653	3,659

Appendix 6

Glossary and abbreviations

AAQC. Ambient air quality criteria.

ACM. Asbestos-containing material; any material that contains 0.5% or greater asbestos content by dry weight (O. Reg. 278/05, s. 1).

AMP. Asbestos Management Program.

actinolite. A mineral that is considered to be asbestos when it occurs in fibrous form.

air samples. Samples collected by drawing a specified volume of air; in this case, at least 2,400 liters of air, through specified sample filters.

amosite. A type of asbestos that becomes airborne easily and is not easily wetted. The removal of insulation or other materials that contain amosite presents an increased risk of exposure to asbestos relative to the removal of chrysotile-containing material.

analysis (defined under the *OHSA* and *EPA*). Methods and procedures used to determine whether material contains asbestos; a material's asbestos content; and the type of asbestos a material contains.

anthophyllite. A type of mineral that is considered to be a form of asbestos when it occurs in fibrous form.

asbestiform. A term used to describe certain silicate minerals that crystallize in fibers.

asbestos. Any of the following asbestiform silicate minerals: actinolite, amosite, anthophyllite, chrysotile, crocidolite, and tremolite.

asbestos bodies. Inhaled asbestos fibers that have become coated with a substance containing protein and iron; also called "ferruginous bodies".

asbestos-containing material. Material that contains 0.5 percent or more asbestos by dry weight; also called "ACM".

asbestos warts. Skin growths that occur when asbestos fibers penetrate the skin; considered harmless by the MOL.

asbestosis. A chronic, restrictive lung disease caused by the inhalation of asbestos fibers.

building (defined under *OHSA* Regulations). Including a structure, vault, chamber, or tunnel and including (without limitation) its electrical, plumbing, heating, and air handling equipment, including rigid duct work of a building or structure.

bulk material samples. Representative samples of homogeneous building materials collected by a competent worker; the minimum number of samples to be collected from an area of homogeneous material as set out under *OHSA* Regulations.

CEPA. *Canadian Environmental Protection Act.*

C of A. Certificate of Approval (issued by the MOE).

chrysotile. A type of asbestos mineral which was most commonly used in building construction.

competent worker. A worker who: is qualified due to knowledge, training, and experience to perform asbestos-related work; is familiar with the *OHSA* and with the provisions of the *OHSA* Regulations that apply to the work; knows of all potential or actual danger to health or safety in the workplace.

construction (defined under the *OHSA*). Including "erection, alteration, repair, dismantling, demolition, structural maintenance, painting, land clearing, earth moving, grading, excavating, trenching, digging, boring, drilling, blasting, or concreting, the installation of any machinery or plant, and any work or undertaking in connection with a project".

constructor (defined by the Act). "A person who undertakes a project for an owner and includes an owner who undertakes all or part of a project by himself or by more than one employer".

crocidolite. A type of asbestos mineral.

EBR. *Environmental Bill of Rights*

ECO. Environmental Commissioner of Ontario

employer (defined under *OHSA*)—"A person who employs one or more workers or contracts for the services of one or more workers. The term includes a contractor or subcontractor".

EPA. *Environmental Protection Act.*

friable. Any material that, when dry, can be crumbled, pulverized, or powdered by hand pressure; material that is crumbled, pulverized, or powdered (O. Reg. 278/05, s. 1).

HEPA filter. A high efficiency particulate aerosol filter that is at least 99.97 percent efficient in collecting a 0.3 micrometer aerosol.

homogeneous material. Material that is uniform in color and texture.

JHSC. Joint Health and Safety Committee, established under section 9 of the *Occupational Health and Safety Act.*

mesothelioma. A rare cancer arising from the surface-lining cells of the pleura and peritoneum.

MAG. Ministry of the Attorney General.

MOE. The Ontario Ministry of the Environment.

MOL. The Ontario Ministry of Labour.

MSDS. Material Safety Data Sheet.

negative air. A term used to refer to the system of air filtration used for controlling airborne asbestos at asbestos removal projects within a building through the maintenance of lower air pressure on the inside of an enclosure than exists on the outside of the enclosure, e.g.on the floor of a building being renovated.

non-friable. Any material that cannot be crumbled, pulverized, or powered by hand pressure; material that is not crumbled, pulverized, or powdered by hand pressure.

NPRI. National Pollutant Release Inventory.

occupier. Has the same meaning as in the *Occupiers' Liability Act;* a person who is in physical possession of premises, or a person who has responsibility for and control over the condition of premises or the activities carried out on the premises; a person who has control over persons allowed to enter the premises, despite the fact that there is more than one occupier of the same premises.

OEL. An occupational exposure limit established under RRO 1990, Reg. 833 (Control of Exposure to Biological or Chemical Agents), O. Reg. 490/09 (Designated Substances), and the *Occupational Health and Safety Act.*

owner (defined under the *OHSA*). A "trustee, receiver, mortgagee in possession, tenant, lessee, or occupier of any lands or premises used or to be used as a workplace, and a person who acts for or on behalf of an owner as an agent or delegate".

OWNERS. The One Window to National Environmental Reporting System, established under the NPRI.

OWRA. *Ontario Water Resources Act.*

peritoneum. The lining of the abdominal cavity and organs.

phase contrast microscopy (PCM). The least expensive and most widely used method of analyzing air samples for asbestos; PCM can be less accurate than Transmission Electron Microscopy (TEM) because all fibers in the sample, regardless of type, are counted.

pleura. The membrane lining the chest cavity and lungs.

pleural plaques. Those areas of fibrous tissue that may calcify or harden; they are not generally associated with disease.

pre-DAR. Pre-demolition/alteration/repair.

qualified asbestos contractor. A contractor that has submitted the appropriate documents for review and been approved by the MOL.

qualified asbestos consultant. A consultant that possesses the knowledge, experience, and credentials to perform asbestos-related work.

RCA. Royal Commission on Matters of Health and Safety Arising from the Use of Asbestos in Ontario.

WHMIS. Workplace Hazardous Material Information System.

WSIB. Workplace Safety and Insurance Board of Ontario.

Appendix 7

The Role of Mirror Laws

In Canada one of the most frustrating conundrums related to preventing and controlling occupational health and environmental problems is the lack of a coherent constitutional framework to regulate trade and economic activities and promote national policy development.

One of the most effective ways of responding to the coordination problems posed by the Canadian Constitution is the passage of mirror laws based on a shared understanding of what needs to be done. Thus if a consensus can be developed about what is required from our federal, provincial, territorial, aboriginal and municipal governments, it should be at least theoretically possible to sit down with other stakeholders and develop a coherent policy and process framework within current constitutional framework. This emphasizes the need to reopen the Canadian Constitution, an untimely proposition during difficult economic and political periods, when disputes about financing health care and transfer payments are evident.

One of the first major mirror laws developed by the federal and provincial governments to regulate important environmental and health and safety risks was the Transportation of Dangerous Goods (TDG). In 1974 the federal government and other developed nations had signed an international TDG treaty. However the federal and provincial governments were unable to agree on how to implement the treaty because of "constitutional buck-passing" (a well-documented phenomena in the Canadian polity since Europeans began to settle Canada in the sixteenth century).

It took a massive train derailment in Mississauga, Ontario, in the fall of 1979 to get politicians, civil servants, and lawyers to take notice. Nearly one hundred thousand people had to be evacuated. The train was carrying a number of containers of chlorine gas but these were not marked properly because there was no legal requirement at the time. In part the problem was that the railways and airports are regulated mainly by the federal government. Similarly the importation of chemicals into Canada is under federal control. However truck transport is regulated by the provinces, as are most workers and workplace hazards. This was the first big test for a tough, new mayor (Hazel McCallion) who showed her mettle and went on to establish a mayoral dynasty that continues today.

This near-tragedy shocked millions of Canadians and put pressure on all levels of government to develop a comprehensive set of interlocking mirror laws that recognized the validity of laws passed by other jurisdictions. Thus in 1984 the Ontario federal government passed an overarching law called the *Transportation of Dangerous Goods Act*. The other Canadian provinces also passed similar laws. The result was that most gaps and loopholes in jurisdiction were eliminated by 1986. By the end of the 1990s, a fairly comprehensive regime had been put in place. In short the situation was a regulatory nightmare and embarrassment; in contrast most other nations had TDG legislation in the late 1970s.

Key precedents for mirror laws in Canada

There are a number of key precedents for mirror laws in Canada, including
- *Canadian Environmental Protection Act, 1999*
- *Species at Risk Act, 2003 (federal)*
- *Transportation of Dangerous Goods Act, 1984*
- Workplace Hazardous Waste Information System, 1986[56]
- *Personal Information Protection and Electronic Documents Act* (abbreviated *PIPEDA*)

Mirror laws provide an opportunity for our federal, provincial, territorial, aboriginal, and municipal governments to sit down with other stakeholders and develop a coherent policy and process framework within current constitutional framework. If developed properly, the framework can avoid constitutional "buck-passing" and arguably provide a chance to ensure that important public policy goals are achieved.

Without doubt mirror laws are an effective and proven way to address gaps and overlaps in the Canadian constitutional framework; however, mirror laws are one of the most underutilized tools in the environmental area since late 1980s.[57]

It is very clear that a new approach is needed to develop national standards similar to WHMIS that address the challenge of controlling hazards such as asbestos and mold in homes and workplaces. The new federal government (elected in May 2011) fully understands the implications of a failure to act on these types of issues. Mirror laws may offer part of the solution to developing a coherent national policy on these types of problems.

Appendix 8

A Proposed Process for Policy and Law Reform

In the early 1970s, Steve Fram, a former senior counsel working in the Policy Development Division of the Ministry of the Attorney General (MAG), was instrumental in nurturing the consensus model for involving stakeholders and government officials in the development of new laws in Ontario between the early 1970s and his retirement from MAG in 1996.[58] Out of this model, the following Ontario laws were subsequently developed:

- *Environmental Bill of Rights, 1993*
- *Class Proceedings Act, 1992*
- *Construction Lien Act*
- *Trespass to Property Act*
- *Occupier's Liability Act*

The model is robust and has many advantages.

The model has also been used at the federal level in Canada. For example the Canadian Commission on Building and Fire Codes (CCBFC) is responsible for developing and updating the National Model Construction Codes.[59] The CCBFC is assisted by nine standing committees and several task groups and working groups comprised of hundreds of volunteer members. The codes are developed and updated using an extensive consensus-based process, involving all sectors of the construction community and the public. This code development process benefits from the research, technical, and administrative support of the NRC. Ongoing development and updating of the National Model Construction Codes is necessary so that future editions reflect improvements in technology, address emerging health and safety issues, and generally continue to meet the evolving needs of the construction industry.

Appendix 9

Environmental Commissioner Of Ontario, Review of Application, R2006003: Application for Review of RRO 1990, Regulation 347 made under the EPA (Review denied by MOE), Prepared by D. McRobert, ECO Annual Report Supplement, 2006-07.

Extract from the Introduction

In June 2006, two applicants requested a review of Regulation 347, RRO 1990 made under the Environmental Protection Act as it pertains to asbestos waste. They contend that asbestos waste should not be defined as a "non-hazardous solid industrial waste" under Regulation 347 and also recommended that the Ministry of the Environment (MOE) take a number of actions. These included the following:

1) MOE should immediately mandate that asbestos should not be disposed in landfills regulated and designed to accept non-hazardous solid waste;

2) MOE should legislate a "cradle to grave" approach for all aspects of the handling and disposing of asbestos wastes;

3) MOE should provide a "single window" approach to upgrade communications and develop legislative and regulatory protocols, procedures,

standards and guidelines for asbestos handling and disposal, along with all health and safety requirements; and

4) the ministry should carry out mandatory random inspections and investigations, without prior notice, of landfills regulated and designed to accept non-hazardous solid waste to ensure that asbestos wastes are being handled at those facilities in the manner required by Regulation 347.

Both applicants were members of a Citizens Liaison Committee (CLC) for a landfill operating in Niagara Region. They expressed concern that asbestos waste is being improperly accepted and buried at the landfill and at other Ontario landfills regulated to accept non-hazardous solid waste.

To support their application, extensive evidence was provided in two volumes. The applicants included copies of sections of a number of regulations administered by MOE and the Ministry of Labour (MOL). In addition, the applicants also included copies of sections of Certificates of Approvals, some related Registry notices, information about the work of their CLC, and correspondence exchanged between the applicants and the MOE.

The application material also included publications and articles from peer-reviewed journals, newspapers, magazines and a number of web sites. Moreover, the applicants provided a copy of a publication issued in 2005 by the Canadian Auto Workers titled, Pure White: Asbestos – A Canadian Scrapbook. One of the publications included in the evidence was by a group of Canadian occupational health and safety (OHS) experts. Their report argues that asbestos is the "most pervasive environmental hazard in the world," and further claim that the substance is responsible for thousands of preventable cancer deaths globally each year.

The applicants contended that by allowing asbestos waste to be regulated under the current weak provisions of Regulation 347, MOE was potentially liable to charges of criminal negligence under the federal Criminal Code because asbestos has been used in the production of dozens of products including: brake and clutch linings and gaskets for cars and trucks; insulation; flooring and shingles; cement; and plastics. They noted that there is a lack of proper enforcement under existing laws and regulations to ensure that these types of products, which sometimes contain asbestos, are handled under the appropriate provisions of Regulation 347. They disputed the argument made by local municipal and MOE officials that "a little bit" of asbestos is deposited in Ontario landfills "now and then" and there is no risk to the public when this happens.

The applicants also questioned why asbestos is a designated substance under legislation administered by the Ministry of Labour but it is not provided special recognition by MOE under Regulation 347 and in its other regulations and policies. As of May 2007, MOL has identified and designated 11 substances.

To raise the profile of their application, the applicants encouraged a number of residents in Niagara Region and some stakeholder groups (e.g. the Occupational Health Clinics for Ontario) to write letters and e-mails to the ECO and express support for the application. Some of the letters were included in the application. Two of the letter-writers suggested that better regulation of asbestos waste and improved mapping of deposits of asbestos wastes in landfills is important because this will facilitate landfill mining in the future. Landfill mining is premised on the concept that future Ontario governments may wish to allow owners of closed or operating landfills to "mine" portions of the landfills to recover valuable recyclable materials such as paper, plastics, aluminum or steel and remove hazardous materials that may threaten groundwater supplies.

References

Alleman, James E., & Mossman, Brooke T. July 1997. Asbestos Revisited. *Scientific American*: 54–57. Retrieved 20 October 2010.

American Cancer Society. What is asbestos? Retrieved January 12, 2010 and October 20, 2010.

Barbalace, Roberta C. 1995. History of Asbestos, www.Environmentalchemistry.com. (1995-10-22). Retrieved October 20, 2010.

Berman, D. Wayne, and Crump, Kenny S. 2003. Technical support document for a protocol to assess asbestos-related risk. Washington DC: U.S. Environmental Protection Agency.

Berry, G., Newhouse, M., and Turok, Mary. 1972. Combined Effect Of Asbestos Exposure And Smoking On Mortality From Lung Cancer In Factory Workers. *The Lancet* 300 (7775): 476.doi:10.1016/S0140-6736 (72) 91867-3.

Bostock, John & Riley, H.T. (Translators). Asbestinon. *The Natural History of Pliny. Vol. IV.* London: Henry G. Bohn. p. 137. 1856. Retrieved October 20, 2010.

Bourdès, Valérie, Boffetta, Paolo and Pisani, Paolo., "Environmental exposure to asbestos and risk of pleural mesothelioma: review and meta-analysis", *European Journal of Epidemiology,* Volume 16, Number 5 / May, 2000

Brophy, J. T., Keith, M.M., Schieman, J.and Cohn, C., "Asbestos pusher to the world: Canada's asbestos legacy kills tens of thousands at home and abroad." *The Straight Goods*, May 15, 2007; http://www.straightgoods. ca/ViewFeature7.cfm?REF=270

California Contractors State License Board. 2001. Consumers Guide to Asbestos. http://www.Mesothelioma-center.com/diagnosis/Mesothelioma-counter.html

Canadian Auto Workers., *Pure White: Asbestos – A Canadian Scrapbook.* (2005) Toronto: Canadian Auto Workers.

Deer, W.A. Howie, R. and Zussman, J. *An Introduction to the Rock-Forming Minerals* (2nd ed.). New York: Longman, 1992.

Dupre, J.S., Mustard, J.F., and Uffin, R.J. 1984. *Report of the Royal Commission on Matters of Health and Safety Arising from the Use of Asbestos in Ontario.* Ontario Ministry of the Attorney General. Toronto, Ontario.

EnvironmentalChemistry.com website. Undated. A Brief History of Asbestos Use and Associated Health Risks. Retrieved November 12, 2010.

Environmental Commissioner of Ontario, Review of EBR Application. *2006–2007 Annual Report Supplement.* pp. 135–147, Toronto: ECO, 2007.

Estrin, D. and Swaigen, J., *Environment on Trial*, 2nd edition, 1978. Toronto: Canadian Environmental Law Association.

European Union. Regulation (EC) No. 1907/2006 of the European Parliament and of the Council of 18 December 2006 concerning the Registration, Evaluation, Authorisation and Restriction of Chemicals (REACH) and establishing a European Chemicals Agency. Publications Office of the European Union. Retrieved October 20, 2010.

European Union. Directive 2003/18/EC of the European Parliament and of the Council of 27 March 2003 amending Council Directive 83/477/ EEC on the protection of workers from the risks related to exposure to asbestos at work. Publications Office of the European Union. Retrieved October 22, 2010.

Government of Australia. 2009. Australian prohibition on use of chrysotile asbestos. Fact Sheet dated 2009-11-09. www.ascc.gov.au. Retrieved October 22, 2009.

Handberg, Sussi. (in Danish). *Asbest – Det kriminelle tidsrum? {Asbestos – The criminal timespan?}* Aalborg, Denmark: Cementarbejdernes Fagforening. p. 9. ISBN 87-983601-0-8, 1990.

Hogg, Peter, *Constitutional Law of Canada*. Toronto: Carswell, 1995; as updated and amended semi-annually.

Home Air Purifier Expert. Undated. *The Complete Guide to Asbestos*. Viewed in December 2007. http://www.home-air-purifier-expert.com/asbestos-msds.html

Industry Canada. Asbestos. CAS No. 1332-21-4. Retrieved October 20, 2010.

Knox, J.F., Doll, R.S. and Hill, I.D. "Cohort Analysis of Changes in Incidence of Bronchial Carcinoma in a Textile Asbestos Factory", *Annals of the New York Academy of Sciences* 132 (Dec 1965).

Ley, Brian. 1999. Diameter of a Human Hair. *The Physics Factbook*™, Edited by Glenn Elert -- Written by his students. http://hypertext-book.com/facts/documents/about.shtml

Lowe, Julian. *U.K. Asbestos - The Definitive Guide, 2004*. London: British Actuaries, 2004. http://www.actuaries.org.uk/files/pdf/proceedings/giro2004/Lowe.pdf

See also http://www.businessinsurance.com/apps/pbcs.dll/article?AID=999920004605

Maines, Rachel. *Asbestos and Fire: Technological Tradeoffs and the Body at Risk*. Rutgers, NJ: Rutgers University Press, 2005.

Marbon, C.A. 2009. Asbestos Risk Assessment. *The Journal of Undergraduate Biological Studies*: 12–24.

Morinaga, Kenji. 2003. Asbestos in Japan. European Conference 2003. Retrieved March 18, 2010.

Mossman, B.T.; Churg, A. 1998. Mechanisms in the Pathogenesis of Asbestosis and Silicosis. *American Journal of Respiratory and Critical Care Medicine*. 157 (5 Pt 1): 1666–80.PMID 9603153.

National Cancer Institute. Undated. Asbestos Exposure and Cancer Risk. www.Cancer.gov. Retrieved December 10, 2011.

Ontario Ministry of the Environment, Guideline C-6, titled the Handling, Transportation and Disposal of Asbestos Waste in Bulk, dated April 1994. MOE: Queen's Printer, 1994.

Ross, Malcolm, and Nolan, Robert P. 2003. History of asbestos discovery and use and asbestos-related disease in context with the occurrence of asbestos within the ophiolite complexes. In Dilek, Yildirim. Ophiolite Concept and the Evolution of Geological Thought. Special

Paper 373. Boulder, Colorado: Geological Society of America. ISBN 0-8137-2373-6. Retrieved November 26, 2009.

San Francisco Department of Public Health. Undated. What are the health effects of asbestos? http://www.dph.sf.ca.us/eh/asbestos/3health_effects.htm

Sass, Robert. The Need to Broaden the Legal Concept of Risk in Workplace Health and Safety, Canadian Public Policy - Analyse de Politiques, Vol. X11:2:286-293, 1986.

Sass, Robert. A Feminist Conception of Injurious Working Conditions: The Birth of Occupational Health and Safety Legislation. October 1998, School of Social Policy Research, University of Regina; http://www.uregina.ca/spr; social.policy@uregina.ca http://ourspace.uregina.ca/bitstream/10294/921/1/occasional_paper_10.pdf

Saxe, D. *Ontario Environmental Protection Act Annotated*. Current to December 2011. Retrieved December 10, 2011. Toronto: Carswell.

Stanton, M.F., and Layard, M. 1978. The carcinogenicity of fibrous minerals. *National Bureau of Standards Special Publication 506*. Based on a Presentation at the Gaithersburg conference of July 1977.

ToxProbe Inc. 2002. *Potential for Occupational and Environmental Exposure to Ten Carcinogens in Toronto*. Report for Toronto Board of Health. March 2002. http://www.toronto.ca/health/pdf/cr_technicalreport.pdf

Toyokuni, S. 2009. Mechanisms of asbestos-induced carcinogenesis. *Nagoya J. Med. Sci. 71* (1–2): 1–10.

Traill, Robert R. 2011. Asbestos as 'toxic short-circuit' optic-fiber for UV within the cell-net:—Likely roles and hazards for secret UV and IR metabolism. *Journal of Physics: Conference Series 329*: 012017.

Udd, John., *A Chronology of Minerals Development in Canada*. National Resources Canada. Ottawa 1998.

U.S. Environmental Protection Agency. Undated. Fact Sheet on Asbestos. http://www.epa.gov/Region06/6pd/asbestos/asbmatl.htm

Voytek P., and Thorslund, Anver T., Mechanisms of Asbestos Carcinogenicity. *J. Amer. College of Toxicology* 9 (5): 541–550, 1990.

Wisconsin Department of Natural Resources. Undated. Asbestos–History and Uses. August 31, 2007. Archived from the original in December 2007. http://dnr.wi.gov/air/compenf/asbestos/histuse.htm

Other Resources - The Controversy over Canada's Asbestos Promotion Policy, 2010 –

Meet Quebec's "Mr. Asbestos" http://www.thestar.com/news/canada/article/742991

Canada's Breathtaking Hypocrisy on Asbestos http://www.slate.com/id/2298185/

"Yes, we have the $25-million," Quebec firm says of asbestos plan http://www.theglobeandmail.com/news/national/quebec/yes-we-have-the-25-million-quebec-firm-says-of-asbestos-plan/article2181160/

Asbestos Critics Refuse to be Converted After Meeting With Industry Power House http://www.brandonsun.com/lifestyles/breaking-news/asbestoscritics-refuse-to-be-converted-after-meeting-with-industry-powerhouse-130583883.html?

Endnotes

1   Dr. Jim Brophy, Dr. Margaret Keith, J. Schieman,RN .and Cohn, C., "Asbestos pusher to the world: Canada's asbestos legacy kills tens of thousands at home and abroad." May 15, 2007
    http://www.straightgoods.ca/ViewFeature7.cfm?REF=270

2   Robert Sass, The Need to Broaden the Legal Concept of Risk in Workplace Health and Safety, Canadian Public Policy - Analyse de Politiques, X11:2:286-293 1986

3   The Workplace Safety and Insurance Board (WSIB) of Ontario includes most of these products on a list of substances it regulates. Business activities regulated by the WSIB include manufacturing asbestos based products such as

asbestos cement cloth

asbestos paper

brake linings

clutch facings

gaskets

insulation

mill board

packing materials

pipe coverings

pipe and tile, asbestos-cement

shingles, boards and sheets, asbestos-cement.

For additional background, see J.S. Dupre, J.F. Mustard, and R.J. Uffin, *Report of the Royal Commission on Matters of Health and Safety Arising from the Use of Asbestos in Ontario.* Ontario Ministry of the Attorney General. Toronto, Ontario. 1984. Page 12.

See: http://www.wsib.on.ca/wsib/wecm.nsf/Public/D50103

4 See The History of Brakes, Brake website: http://www.brakewarehouse.com/brkewrh-sefaqs.htm

- 1902 Arthur Raymond and Arthur Law form Royal Equipment Co.
- 1906 Woven brake linings are introduced by Royal.
- 1908 Asbestos brake linings are introduced.
- 1916 Royal Equipment becomes Raybestos.
- 1920 Hydraulic brakes are appearing on new cars, replacing mechanical brakes.
- 1969 Front disc brakes are growing in popularity. Greater forces and higher pressures require proportioning valves to reduce hydraulic pressure to the rear drums. Bendix introduces "anti-skid" (now known as ABS).
  First production by Tokico of rear calipers with Lucas load-sensitive adjusters.
- 1974 The Girling Colette, the most successful fist type caliper design throughout the world went into production in Europe for Renault and Lancia and in Japan for Honda.
- 1975 Congress passes the Corporate Average Fuel Economy law forcing automakers to make lighter cars. Brake components start to get smaller.
- 1986 Anti-lock brake systems are available on the BMW and Corvette and some full-size GM and Ford vehicles. First introduction of a low-cost ABS system in Ford Escort.
- 1987 Year of record 100 million Colette calipers produced worldwide.
- 1988 Asbestos-free pads are entering the marketplace. Kevlar formulas introduced to replace asbestos.
- 1994 ABS brakes becoming standard equipment on most cars. Most trucks have rear-wheel antilock brakes.
- 1999 Brakewarehouse.com formed as a division of Dynamic Automotive Distributors, Inc.
- 2000 Ceramic-enhanced friction formulas become popular.
- 2002 ABS brakes become standard equipment on entry-level cars. Trucks have front and rear ABS now as standard equipment. 4-wheel disc braking systems are the rule instead of the exception.

5 *The Complete Guide to Asbestos.* Viewed in December 2007. http://www.home-air-purifier-expert.com/asbestos-msds.html

6　See San Francisco Department of Public Health. What are the health effects of asbestos? http://www.dph.sf.ca.us/eh/asbestos/3health_effects.htm

7　http://www.labour.gov.on.ca/english/hs/asbestos/index.html

8　See website: Mesothelioma & Asbestos Exposure Information http://www.consultwebs.com/mesothelioma-asbestos/mesothelioma_asbestos_faqs.html

9　See, for example, http://www.btinternet.com/~ibas/lka_ards.htm The author points out that the British courts have accepted latency periods as short as ten years.

10　The Royal Commission on Matters of Health and Safety Arising from the Use of Asbestos in Ontario considered all aspects of the asbestos problem. After considering all available data, the commission concluded I its final report (Chapter 9, Page 585) that: "... The risk to occupants from asbestos in buildings is a small fraction of the risks faced by workers exposed to asbestos under the 1 f/cc control limit for chrysotile (the current exposure limit for industrial asbestos use in Ontario). It is less than 1/50 as great as the risk of commuting by car to and from those buildings. In concluding that this risk is insignificant, we conclude that the risk does not pose a public health problem. While asbestos has caused serious health problems for workers and may present a problem for building maintenance, renovation, construction, and demolition workers, we conclude that it does not pose a significant problem for the general occupants of a building, except in the three situations outlined in section D of this chapter, namely: (I) the occupant is in the immediate vicinity of work that disturbs friable asbestos-containing insulation; (ii) the occupant is within the range of air circulation of work that disturbs friable asbestos-containing insulation; (iii) significant quantities of friable asbestos-containing insulation have fallen onto building surfaces and are being disturbed."

11　The three situations are outlined in section D of chapter 9 of the RCA Report, namely: (I) the occupant is in the immediate vicinity of work that disturbs friable asbestos-containing insulation; (ii) the occupant is within the range of air circulation of work that disturbs friable asbestos-containing insulation; (iii) significant quantities of friable asbestos-containing insulation have fallen onto building surfaces and are being disturbed." Moreover, in the overview to Chapter 9, page 548 the RCA states: "... We conclude that it is rarely necessary to take corrective action in buildings containing asbestos insulation in order to protect the general occupants of those buildings. On the other hand, construction, demolition, renovation, maintenance, and custodial workers in asbestos containing-buildings may be exposed to significant fibre levels and may, during their work, cause elevated fibre levels for nearby occupants."

12 Valérie Bourdès, Paolo Boffetta and Paola Pisani, "Environmental exposure to asbestos and risk of pleural mesothelioma: review and meta-analysis", *European Journal of
Epidemiology,* Volume 16, Number 5 / May, 2000. Here is an excerpt: "Abstract - A
number of epidemiological studies have addressed the risk of pleural mesothelioma
from environmental (household and neighborhood) exposure to asbestos, but no overall risk estimate is available. We reviewed the epidemiological studies on risk of pleural mesothelioma and household or neighborhood exposure to asbestos. We identified
eight relevant studies; most were conducted in populations with relatively high exposure levels. We combined the risk estimates in a meta-analysis based on the random-
effects model. The relative risks (RRs) of pleural mesothelioma for household exposure
ranged between 4.0 and 23.7, and the summary risk estimate was 8.1 (95% confidence
interval [CI]: 5.3–12). For neighborhood exposure, RRs ranged between 5.1 and 9.3
(with a single RR of 0.2) and the summary estimate was 7.0 (95% CI: 4.7–11). This
review suggests a substantial increase in risk of pleural mesothelioma following high
environmental exposure to asbestos; however, the available data are insufficient to
estimate the magnitude of the excess risk at the levels of environmental exposure commonly encountered by the general population in industrial countries."

13 See David Estrin and John Swaigen, Environment on Trial, 1978, p. 89 The regulation
was titled the Asbestos Mining and Milling National Emission Standards Regulation,
SOR/77-514 made under the CAA.

14 CEPA, Asbestos Mines and Mills Release Regulations SOR/90-341. Section 3 states: 3.

(1) The concentration of asbestos fibres contained in any gases that the owner or operator of a mine or mill may release into the ambient air from

(a) crushing, drying or milling operations,

(b) dry rock storage, or

(c) primary dry drilling operations in an open pit

at that mine or mill, shall not exceed two asbestos fibres per normal cubic centimetre
of the gases.

(2) The concentration of asbestos fibres referred to in paragraph (1)(a) or (b) shall
be measured dry and undiluted, under normal operating conditions, in accordance with the applicable method described in Standard Reference Methods for
Source Testing: Measurements of Emissions of Asbestos from Mining and Milling
Operations; Department of Fisheries and Environment Report EPS-1-AP-75-1
dated December 1976, as amended from time to time.

(3) The concentration of asbestos fibres referred to in paragraph (1)(c) shall be measured dry and undiluted, under normal operating conditions, in accordance with the
method described in Standard Reference Methods for Source Testing: Measurement

of Emissions of Asbestos from Asbestos Mining and Milling Operations Method S-3 Sampling of Drill Baghouse Exhaust Emissions, Department of Fisheries and the Environment Canada Report EPS-1-AP-75-1A dated March 1978, as amended from time to time.

(4) Where Method S.1 described in the Report referred to in subsection (2) is used,

(a) three release measurements shall be made;

(b) each release measurement shall be made during a minimum continuous process operational period of 30 minutes;

(c) the asbestos fibres on each filter shall be counted by two qualified persons, one counting the odd numbered sectors and the other counting the even numbered sectors;

(d) each release measurement shall be determined by taking the arithmetic average of the two sets of fibre counts conducted in accordance with paragraph (c); and

(e) the concentration of asbestos fibres contained in gases released into the ambient air shall be the arithmetic average of the three measurements conducted in accordance with paragraphs (a) to (d).

(5) Where Method S.2 described in the Report referred to in subsection (2) is used,

(a) one release measurement shall be made;

(b) the asbestos fibres on each filter shall be counted by two qualified persons, one counting the odd numbered sectors and the other counting the even numbered sectors; and

(c) the release measurement shall be determined by taking the arithmetic average of the two sets of fibre counts conducted in accordance with paragraph (b).

(6) Where Method S.3 described in the Report referred to in subsection (3) is used,

(a) three release measurements shall be made;

(b) each release measurement shall be made during a period of continuous active drilling;

(c) the asbestos fibres on each filter shall be counted by two qualified persons, one counting the odd numbered sectors and the other counting the even numbered sectors;

(d) each release measurement shall be determined by taking the arithmetic average of the two sets of fibre counts conducted in accordance with paragraph (c); and

(e) the concentration of asbestos fibres contained in gases released into the ambient air shall be the arithmetic average of the three measurements conducted in accordance with paragraphs (a) to (d). SOR/93-231, s. 2; SOR/94-364, s. 2.

15 http://www.ec.gc.ca/inrp-npri/default.asp?lang=En&n=C3FF94C3-1

16 http://www.ene.gov.on.ca/envision/monitoring/monitoring.htm

17 MOE, Step by Step Guideline for Emission Calculation, Record Keeping and Reporting for Airborne Contaminant Discharge. Dated April 2001.

18 The February 2008 amendment has removed substances that are required to be reported through other federal/provincial regulations and has de-listed substances that present minimal risk, if any, to the environment and human health. In addition the 2008 amendment has eliminated some duplicate reporting requirements. The present amendments to O. Reg. 127/01 Step by Step Guideline will de-list all of the substances listed under O. Reg. 127/01 except for acetone which will be (for reporting year 2007) the single substance under O. Reg. 127/01 to be reported through One Window National Environmental Reporting System (OWNERS).

Facilities need to report these substances if, in 2010, they were manufactured, processed, or otherwise used at the facility in a quantity of ten tons or more and if employees (including contractors) worked 20,000 hours or more.

http://www.ec.gc.ca/inrp-npri/default.asp?lang=En&n=C3FF94C3-1

O. Reg. 127/01 sets out three different sets of screening criteria for determining what monitoring and reporting each facility must undertake. Facilities subject to Ontario's Regulation that are also required to report to Environment Canada under the National Pollutant Release Inventory (NPRI) must provide the same air emissions data to the MOE. The MOE also introduced two lists of contaminants not covered by NPRI. Under O. Reg. 127/01 specific dischargers of friable asbestos including certain types of mining and manufacturing plants are required to report to the MOE. These dischargers are required to follow the MOE's guide titled Step by Step Guideline for Emission Calculation, Record Keeping and Reporting for Airborne Contaminant Discharge, dated April 2001.

19 RRO 1990, Reg. 347, ss. 17(16).

20 This section is based on Supplement version. For references, see endnoted version and reference package.

21 Communication to David McRobert from George Rocoski (Director, Central Region, MOE). January 18, 2008.

22 *R.* v. *Oebele Mast.* Unreported decision. June 21, 2005. Ont. Prov. Court, Sarnia. For a summary, see http://www.legalemissions.net/2005_Edition.pdf

(TRIAL) (June 21/05) – Sarnia

The defendant was found guilty, after trial, of operating a waste management system without a C of A, contrary to s. 27(1)(a) of the EPA. During the fall of 2002, the defendant was hired to remove and dispose of asbestos waste at a senior citizens' home which was undergoing renovations. He bagged some of the asbestos waste and transported it to asbestos waste bins in London which were owned by a disposal company, without notifying the company and without completing manifests for the loads of waste. Some of the asbestos waste was mixed with demolition waste from the project and deposited in bins of demolition waste for disposal by a company not licensed to haul asbestos waste. Although the defendant had once owned a corporation which held a C of A to operate a waste management system for the transportation of asbestos waste, that corporation had been dissolved in 1994. The defendant was fined $45,000.

23 D. Saxe. Ontario *EPA* Annotated. Current to December 2008, p. R-293.

24 D. Saxe. Ontario *EPA* Annotated. Current to December 2008, p. R-293.

25 In 2003, the City of London charged $300 per ton. See its Waste Management Fees report.
    In 2007, Timmins increased its fees to $75 per ton.

26 See Environmental Commissioner of Ontario, Annual Report Supplement, 2006–2007. (Toronto: Queen's Printer, November 2007). Hereinafter: ECO 06 07 Supplement, p. 146.

27 The handling of this application was reviewed in the ECO's 2006–2007 Annual Report Supplement (pp. 135–147).
    As noted in the ECO's review, at the time the ECO did not believe that it would be appropriate or practical for the MOE to treat most residual asbestos-containing products (such as brake linings, used roof shingles, etc.) as hazardous wastes under Regulation 347. The ECO stated that "while the risks to the environment and human health posed by asbestos in commercial goods and other products are difficult to evaluate, it is doubtful, based on current evidence, that these risks warrant treatment of these products as hazardous wastes under the Regulation."

28 *The Complete Guide to Asbestos.* Viewed in December 2007.
    http://www.home-air-purifier-expert.com/asbestos-msds.html

29 *The Complete Guide to Asbestos.* Viewed in December 2007.
    http://www.home-air-purifier-expert.com/asbestos-msds.html

30 Health experts and researchers often report the number of fibers in a milliliter (mL) (equivalent to a cubic centimeter [cm^3]) of air rather than in a cubic meter of air. Using this metric, there typically would be 0.00001 fibers of asbestos in the ambient air of rural areas since there are one million cm^3 (or one million mL) in a cubic meter.

31 *The Complete Guide to Asbestos.* Viewed in December 2007.
    http://www.home-air-purifier-expert.com/asbestos-msds.html

32 ToxProbe Inc. Report for Toronto Board of Health. March 2002. p. 8.

33 Note that 1 gram is equal to 1,000,000 nanograms (ng).

34 *The Complete Guide to Asbestos.* Viewed in December 2007.
    http://www.home-air-purifier-expert.com/asbestos-msds.html

35 MOE, *Proposed Guideline for the Implementation of Air Standards in Ontario*. Ontario Ministry of the Environment. June 2004.

36 MOE, Proposed Guideline for the Implementation of Air Standards in Ontario. Ontario Ministry of the Environment. June 2004. The proposed amendments also include the phase-in of a set of new U.S. Environmental Protection Agency (EPA) air dispersion models (i.e., AERMOD, ISCST Prime and SCREEN3) to replace the models currently used in Ontario (e.g., the thirty-year old Reg. 346 model). These new models can more accurately predict ground level air concentrations by considering all atmospheric conditions and incorporating site-specific meteorological data that can significantly influence modeled results. They also include improved methods for dealing with complex terrain and account for atmospheric deposition. In accordance with the new AAQCs, these models will allow the user to predict air concentrations for different averaging times and can do so under variable emission rate scenarios. When air dispersion modelling results indicate that ground level air concentrations resulting from a facility's emissions do not meet the appropriate AAQC, a risk-based decision making process will be implemented. With consideration paid to the magnitude and frequency of the exceedence, the basis of the standard, technological alternatives, cost considerations, and community/stakeholder consultation, a management plan can be developed to address the exceedence.

37 MOE, Summary of O. Reg. 419/05 Standards and Point of Impingement Guidelines & Ambient Air Quality Criteria (AAQCs), 2005. (Sorted by CAS Number) http://www.ene.gov.on.ca/envision/gp/2424e05.pdf, p. 9.

38 MOE, Summary of O. Reg. 419/05 Standards and Point of Impingement Guidelines & Ambient Air Quality Criteria (AAQCs), 2005. (Sorted by CAS Number) http://www.ene.gov.on.ca/envision/gp/2424e05.pdf, p. 3

39 Until 1970, the technique for measuring asbestos concentration at indoor work sites involved the use of impinger sampling followed by the counting of particles using optical microscopy. Changes in international practice by the late 1960s resulted in the redefining of asbestos from simple particle counts to fibres longer than 5 microns and with a length to diameter ratio of at least 3.0. With this new definition and the continued use of counting fibres with an optical microscope, the Ontario government adopted the new standard of 5 fibres/cc recommended by the ACGIH in 1970.

40 See "Large fines for asbestos infractions", June 4, 2007, Hazardous Management Magazine, http://www.hazmatmag.com/issues/ISarticle.asp?id=69772&story_id=&issue=06042007&PC=
Two Ontario companies were fined recently under the province's Occupational Health and Safety Act for failing to provide workers removing asbestos with appropriate personal protective equipment.

Suncor Energy Products Inc., a Toronto-based company operating a refinery in Sarnia, Ontario, was fined $25,000 after pleading guilty, as a constructor, to failing to ensure friable material discovered during work, that was not referred to in a previously-prepared asbestos report, was reported to the Ministry of Labour (MOL), both orally and in a written report, as required by subsection 7(6) of the Asbestos on Construction Projects and in Buildings and Repair Operations Regulation (RRO 1990, Reg. 838), contrary to subsection 23(1) of the Act.

Suncor was also fined $100,000 after pleading guilty, as a constructor, to failing to ensure workers were provided with protective equipment that included a respirator with supplied air, positive pressure full face piece respirator for a Type 3 asbestos removal, as required by clause 14(5)(viii) of the regulation, contrary to clause 23(1)(b) of the Act. Tornado Insulation Limited in London, Ontario was fined $50,000 after pleading guilty, as an employer, to the same offence.

Between March 9 and 12, 2005, workers removed insulation and other material from heat exchangers and a stripper change drum. On March 11, 2005, a concern was raised that material on the stripper change drum contained asbestos.

Suncor sent the material for testing and it was confirmed that the material contained asbestos. However, Suncor failed to notify the MOL of the asbestos, both orally and by submitting a required written report in a timely fashion. And both Suncor and Tornado Insulation failed to ensure workers wore appropriate personal protective equipment when removing the material after the suspected asbestos was discovered and after it was confirmed.

41 Even if there is no asbestos, the owner still needs to write a report stating that no asbestos is present.

42 According to articles in *Hazardous Materials Management Magazine* in 2004 and 2005.

43 Communication to David McRobert from George Rocoski (Director, Central Region, MOE). January 18, 2008.

44 Communication to David McRobert from George Rocoski (Director, Central Region, MOE). January 18, 2008.

45 See endnote 14.

46 Communication to David McRobert from George Rocoski (Director, Central Region, MOE). January 18, 2008.

47 http://www.wsib.on.ca/wsib/wopm.nsf/Public/160205
Claims for asbestosis are allowed by the WSIB when it is established that the worker
  • has a diagnosis of asbestosis, and
  • worked in any mining, milling, manufacturing, assembling, construction, repair, alteration, maintenance, or demolition process involving the generation of airborne asbestos fibers
  • was exposed to asbestos dust for at least two years.

The legislative requirements of sections 15(5) and 15(6) of the Workplace Safety and Insurance Act for two years of asbestos dust exposure in Ontario apply to this policy.

48 Ibid.

49 California Contractors State License Board. *Consumers Guide to Asbestos.* 2001. p. 4.

50 http://www.Mesothelioma-center.com/diagnosis/Mesothelioma-counter.html

51 See San Francisco Department of Public Health. What are the health effects of asbestos? http://www.dph.sf.ca.us/eh/asbestos/3health_effects.htm

52 ToxProbe Inc. Report for Toronto Board of Health. March 2002. p. 8.

53 ToxProbe Inc. Report for Toronto Board of Health. March 2002. p. 8.

54 Communication to David McRobert from George Rocoski (Director, Central Region, MOE). January 18, 2008.

55 Communication to David McRobert from George Rocoski (Director, Central Region, MOE). January 18, 2008.

56 This is an umbrella system and was implemented through the passage of amendments to a wide range of federal and provincial laws in the late 1980s.

57 David McRobert adds the following observation:

For nearly twenty years, I taught environmental law at York University and I would encourage students to prepare papers on how mirror laws could be used to address environmental problems such as climate change, energy and water conservation, waste reduction, toxics avoidance and reduction—to name only a few. I remain convinced of their efficacy although I find that I am constantly rebuffed by my colleagues in environmental law. In 1995 and 1996, my former students and I prepared a submission for Charles Caccia, the former Minister of the Environment and Chair of the Standing Committee on Environment and Sustainable Development, urging him to find ways to incorporate the mirror law concept into what became known eventually as the Species at Risk Act, 2003, and consider the idea for CEPA reforms. We were delighted when mirror law concepts were incorporated into both laws.

58 Steve was David McRobert's mentor and friend when David was an articling student in the Ontario Ministry of the Attorney General, 1988–1989. Steve was a senior lawyer who oversaw the students working in the Policy Development Division of MAG, where he was based.

59 National Model Construction Code Documents; www.nationalcodes.nrc.gc.ca; http://www.nationalcodes.ca/eng/questions.shtml

www.ingramcontent.com/pod-product-compliance
Lightning Source LLC
Chambersburg PA
CBHW051340170526
45166CB00002B/895